The
COSMOPO
Guide to
Online Dating

The
COSMOPOLITAN
Guide to
Online Dating

A Practical Guide for Dating Divas

GEORGIA BARLOW

BOOKS

First published in Great Britain in 2009 by
JR Books, 10 Greenland Street, London NW1 0ND
www.jrbooks.com

A catalogue record for this book is available from the British Library.

ISBN 978-1-906217-98-3

1 3 5 7 9 10 8 6 4 2

Printed by Thomson Litho Ltd, East Kilbride, Scotland

Contents

Introduction

Feel the fear and . . . stop being such a wuss!

Whether you're taking a sneaky peek at this book between the shelves of your local bookshop, it's been bestowed upon you by a 'well-meaning' coupled up friend or you've secretly ordered a copy online, the chances are you're in the market for a little romance right now (whether it be a flirtation, a fling or a future husband) and you're toying with the idea of trying your luck online.

Perhaps you're sick of wasted nights spent trawling bars hoping to find a soulmate only to find yourself fighting off sleazeballs. Or worse, falling prey to said sleazeballs courtesy of last night's beer goggles (last night he looked like Vernon Kaye; this morning he looks like Peter Kaye). Or maybe, like me, you work in an office full of women so it's slim pickings at the water cooler or all your coupled up mates have given up playing cupid because you're just too damn fussy ('But he had a *Barbra Streisand CD* in his collection – and it wasn't his mum's!').

But let me guess, you're not completely convinced, are you? After all, online dating is the preserve of geeks, freaks and desperados, right? And you're . . . well, you're no minger. In fact you look pretty hot in *that* dress when you've got your mascara on and your hair's behaving. I mean you could get a man if you really wanted, you just haven't found anyone up to the job. Besides, even if there are other 'normal' people on there, what would your cool mates think? Then of course there's the hideous business of putting pictures of yourself online and trying to write a witty paragraph about how great you are. Oh, and we haven't even got to the spending-the-evening-with-a-complete-stranger/potential-serial-killer bit . . .

Okay, here's the thing. *Nobody* wants to internet date. Until they try it. I know I didn't. A couple of years ago, I felt that signing up to a dating website would be an official declaration that I can't get a man – the dating equivalent of going to AA. My name's Georgia and I can't get a boyfriend. I would no longer be able to use the line 'I don't need a man, I'm happy being commitment-free' in response to the question, 'So, how come you're still single?' I'd have to resort to the honest answer instead ('Because I can only manage meaningless flings with inappropriate losers'), or the really honest answer ('None of your goddamn business!').

Back then, none of my friends were internet dating. For them, love had come knocking at the door. They hadn't resorted to bribing it with a £20 credit card payment or touting for it with a full advertising campaign. And I did not want to be the first.

So, what convinced me to change my mind? If I'm really honest, it was three little words: Checked. Shirt. Boy. I had sworn that if one more well-meaning friend suggested I try love online, I'd tell them where to stick their cupid's arrow. Then my friend Sarah called. 'So, you know Checked Shirt Boy from John's party who you said was your perfect man? Guess what? He's got a girlfriend', she chirped. 'Er, great Sah. Cheers. And you're telling me this because . . . ?' I'd replied irritably. 'Well he met her online. He's been internet dating – and all his mates are, too!' Now call me shallow but for me that changed everything. It's like being told Jude Law has started going down your dodgy local pub – well, you'd at least go and have a look, wouldn't you?

Anyway, just after Sarah's phone call I found myself facing a single girl's worst nightmare – a Friday night in by myself. My flatmate Lucy was on a romantic weekend away and my new pulling partner had bailed out on me at the last minute. While I was sitting on the sofa feeling sorry for myself and contemplating nipping to the shop to buy a family-sized bar of Dairy Milk before the start of *Corrie*, I caught a glimpse of my laptop glistening in the corner of the living room. Were there really loads of sexy, single men like Checked Shirt Boy inside that computer, looking for a date? There was only one thing for it – I poured myself a glass of wine and reached for the laptop. And there began my foray into internet dating.

So, was that it? Did I go skipping off into the sunset with The One before my three-month subscription expired? Um, no, but I did get emails from ten men by *Corrie* End of Part One and by the end of the bottle of Pinot I had been invited to a Kings of Leon gig by Another Checked Shirt . . . and all from the comfort of my own sofa . . . with pyjamas on...and hair removal cream on my top lip. What more could a girl ask for damnit?

What this book is *not*

You see, I'm not here to glamorise this online dating lark

or to suggest it is the failsafe fast-track route to finding a husband. This is not one of those stuck-in-the-50s self-help books that claim to hold the secret formula for finding Mr Right in a flash. If I knew that, do you really think I'd have spent the early part of my thirties writing about my hapless and colourful love-life as *Cosmo*'s Sex & The Single Girl columnist (aka 'a low-rent Carrie Bradshaw in Converse')? Besides, if the truth be known I don't believe in this Mr Right/The One business. But before you slam this book down in dismay at my cynicism, please hear me out. I don't believe in The One because I believe there are thousands of Ones out there. And actually I don't think there's any harm in a few dalliances with Mr Wrongs along the way. It's character building. Plus it helps you to understand what it is you really want.

So I'm not here to dictate some ridiculous set of rules to assist you in trapping your dream man ('Pretend you don't like him'/'Wait three days to text him back'/'Don't sleep with him until date ten') or anything daft like that.

Nor am I here to plug the benefits of online dating in a bid to get you to part with all your hard-earned cash and sign-up for life membership with some new site I'm backing.

So what *is* this book then?

I'm just here to tell you, with an honest, unbiased opinion, about an easy, accessible way to meet/flirt with/date/maybe even fall in love with . . . men (or women if that's what you prefer) because I've been doing this thing on and off for a while now so I do speak from experience.

And when I say experience, I'm not preaching to you

from the higher ground here. I'm talking about the good, the bad *and* the ugly. So at least where I can't be a good example, you can always rely on me to be a horrible warning. Think of me as the friend who makes you feel better about yourself when you've done something really stupid because you know she's already done worse; the one who you ask for advice before you send that text, not because she always makes the right move but because she's the one who *did* send the text, regretted it and will tell you the consequences in no uncertain terms so you don't have to make the same mistake.

But of course not even I can have made every mistake in the book (so many mistakes to make, so little time) so I don't expect you to rely on me as the sole fountain of knowledge on this. Which is why I have spent the past few months speaking to hundreds of fellow online daters from across the land to uncover the no-holds-barred truth about what really happens when you log on to find love. But don't let the weird and wonderful tales in Chapter 12 put you off without reading the real-life fairytale endings in Chapter 13. After all, even your average fairytale princess has to kiss a few frogs before her prince shows up.

To give you a taster of what's to come, here are some of the highlights and lowlights you might expect to encounter on the rollercoaster that is online dating. The question is are you up for what could be the ride of your life?

10 reasons internet dating rocks . . .

1. You can pull ten men in ten minutes . . .
2. . . . on a Tuesday lunchtime . . .

3. . . . from the comfort of your own sofa . . .
4. . . . while wearing your dressing gown . . .
5. . . . and watching *Grey's Anatomy*
6. Every guy you meet is (allegedly) single and looking to meet someone. No time wasters.
7. You can establish whether he ticks the most important boxes (for example, wants kids, can put up a shelf . . .) before you even meet.
8. You get to make your first impression online with the aid of spell-check, Photoshop and time to prepare those 'off-the-cuff' one-liners.
9. You can spend more time having fun with your friends at the weekends and save your flirting for when there's nothing on telly midweek!
10. You don't need to feel ashamed that you secretly Googled him – all his personal details are there on show to satisfy your inner stalker.

10 harsh truths you should know now

1. He will look nothing like his picture (nine out of ten times he will look worse, but it's worth going for ten dates just to hold out for the one who is a pleasant surprise).
2. The one who is a pleasant surprise is most likely to be the one out of ten who *doesn't* call. He's probably got a waiting list. Move on.
3. Falling in love via email is no guarantee you'll fall in love on the date. Chemistry is a powerful thing. Meet face to face as soon as you feel comfortable.
4. Your 'fans' page will never be in the same league

as your 'favourites' page. Don't take it personally.

5. He's not going to take himself off the site after one good date with you. Give him a break. He's paid good money for this and he doesn't want to count his chickens with you yet . . . or put all his eggs in one basket (and any other poultry analogies he can think of!).

6. Nobody said online dating *wasn't* for geeks, freaks and desperados . . . just that it wasn't *only* for geeks, freaks and desperados. Prepare to meet some nutters – just like the real world.

7. The competition is high. There are a lot of lovely ladies' profiles out there but stop comparing yourself to them. There are plenty of men to go around.

8. You will click on men who don't click back and have emails ignored. Don't get hung up on this. He hasn't got time to date everyone. Move on and never chase – he knows where to find you.

9. There is a fine line between the glass of wine that loosens your tongue on a nerve-wracking first date and the one that loosens your morals. Know your limits.

10. Your profiles might suggest you're a 100 per cent match, but don't get carried away. If you take out the white lies and 'minor' embellishments you've both made you are probably more like a 50 per cent match. No two people are 100 per cent match, 100 per cent of the time.

CHAPTER 1

Before You Log On

Fasten your seat belt

A word of warning: If you think online dating sounds like the laid-back, lazy way to find love, you might want to fasten your seat belt. Don't forget the online part is only the half of it. The idea is that you do actually log off, leave the house and go on real dates. Yes, that's right, in person, without a username and computer screen to hide behind. What's more, the offers can come pretty thick and fast once you get into the swing of things. Before you know it you've got three guys you don't fancy badgering you for a second date and a guy you really do fancy ignoring you since your first date three days ago. Not to mention the fact you've 'accidentally' booked back-to-back dates with different men every night next week because you stupidly logged on after a bottle of wine on Saturday night and it all seemed like a good idea at the time.

It's like *Sex and the City* (minus the Manolo Blahniks)

One minute your love life's cruising along in the slow lane, the next minute you're on a rollercoaster of highs and lows, twists and turns. Suddenly you're living out your own version of *Sex and the City*, except in your version there's none of this 'long lunches and designer shoe shopping' business to ease the stress. You've actually got to fit in a full-time job, too. Plus you don't have a team of professional make-up artists sorting out the bags under your eyes. All those late nights combined with pre-date nerves and post-date text anxiety is enough to make even the most accomplished dating diva want to dive into her pyjamas and spend a night in on the sofa with a cup of cocoa.

Things can get pretty intense. One minute you're feeling more popular than a box of Krispy Kremes at a Weightwatchers meeting ('I've had seven emails in the past hour!'), the next minute your ego's packing its bags and heading off to the nearest nunnery ('Why hasn't he added me to his favourites? He's not even that hot!'). If regular dating is the equivalent of watching an episode of *Sex and the City* on TV once a week, online dating is like watching the entire Series 1 to 6 boxed set plus the movie in one weekend marathon. So, if you're *not* on top form – whether you're nursing a broken heart, feeling vulnerable from a past relationship or in the middle of a crisis of confidence – you could be in for a bumpy ride.

Are you 'date' ready?

Before you whip out your credit card and sign the next three months of your life away, it's time for a little self-assessment:

Are you over him?

The fact you're even reading this book suggests that if you are post-break-up you're at least over the worst of it (the bit where you've been wearing your pyjamas for so long they would be able to stand up by themselves, you're listening to James Blunt on repeat as a non-invasive form of self-harm and you're sleeping (on average about 17 hours a day) beneath a blanket of tissues and chocolate wrappers) because at that stage, the only men likely to get a look-in in your life are Ben & Jerry.

But break-ups can be deceptive. Just because you made it through to lunchtime without crying/calling him/lapsing into a fantasy about winning him back, does not necessarily mean you're ready to dive back into the dating pool head first. Online dating is not a cure for heartbreak. First, you need to ask yourself if you're *really* ready to meet someone else. If your motives for signing up are any of the following, the answer is probably no:

'I can't face the idea of being single again.'

'I want to make him jealous.'

'He's with someone else so I should be with someone else, too.'

'I need to know I'm still attractive to men.'

3

'I need a distraction to stop me thinking about him.'

'I want to find someone just like him.'

'I'm the only one of my friends who's single now.'

Men on . . . girls with EX-cess baggage

'There's only one thing more off-putting than a girl with "ex" issues – and that's a drunk girl with "ex" issues. I'd been chatting to Amy* on email for a couple of weeks and she sounded great. We shared an offbeat sense of humour and love of gigs so I invited her to see a band for our first date and arranged to meet her in a pub beforehand. I wasn't disappointed when she walked through the door – she was gorgeous! She was really chatty and open too so the conversation flowed easily. Because I was a bit nervous I was drinking faster than usual and noticed that she was matching me pint for pint. I like a girl who's not afraid to drink pints so I thought that was quite cool at first but about halfway through pint three the alcohol must have hit her and the conversation took a nose-dive.

It started when I mentioned a gig I'd been to. It turned out Amy had been to the same gig with her ex. It also turned out that her "cheating scumbag of an ex" had only been "ex" for about a month. To cut a long story short Amy's mood went on a downward spiral. It began with hatred of the ex (accompanied by tears), which quickly moved on to hatred of all men and eventually to hatred of all men including me! The next thing I know, Amy stands up, starts hurling abuse at me for no apparent reason and storms out. The couple at the next table who had heard the whole thing, asked me if I was okay and invited me to join them. But ten minutes later, Amy storms back in again and starts flailing her arms around and screaming at me for not following her to see if she was okay. At this point the bouncer heads over to see what the problem is and tries to pull Amy away from the table. Amy loses her footing, bangs her head on the table and knocks herself out for a second and I end up having to carry her out with the bouncer and take her home in a taxi.

The next day Amy called me, absolutely mortified about what had happened. Apparently she was completely heartbroken about the ex and that was the first time she'd been out for weeks. She thought I might be able to help her get over him. Great! My advice is if you're not over your ex you shouldn't be going on dates. Simple as.' Simon, 26, Norfolk

Would YOU go on a date with you?

If online dating is not a cure for heartbreak, neither is it a quick-fix solution to a self-esteem slump. For although you will probably get more male attention in one week than you normally would in a month, it stands to reason you will also be in the firing line for more rejection. This is nothing personal but it's more likely to feel that way if you're in any doubts about your own self-worth to begin with.

Having spoken to a gazillion single men while researching this book, it came to my attention that 'happy', 'positive', 'independent' and 'confident' were somewhere at the top of the tick-list for most. And sadly, writing that you're 'happy, positive, independent and confident' in your profile will not fool anyone for long if it isn't coming from the heart. It comes down to that age-old cliché: if you don't love yourself how can you expect anyone else to?

The irony is, you will get the most out of online dating if you're happy being single. If you're unhappy on your own, the problem is within and no man is going to change that. The only person who can really super-charge your self-esteem is you, so try looking at the root of the issue and asking yourself why you don't feel date-worthy. If it's an ongoing issue, speak to friends or a professional. If, on the other hand you're just suffering from a temporary blip or a bout of pre-dating jitters, check out the crash-course in confidence on p. 36.

Learn from your mistakes

So, you're pretty happy with your lot and the single life is sweet, but someone to share the good times would make it that little bit sweeter, right? The icing on the cake, perhaps? But hold on, haven't you been here before? What happened last time and the time before? The icing melted? Then now might be a good time to rethink the recipe you've been using (sorry, I've started this baking analogy and I'm damn well going to finish it). After all, like a cake, a successful relationship is all about the right balance of ingredients. But unlike a cake, the recipe that worked for your granny is not necessarily going to work for you.

Unfortunately, you need to work out the right mixture for yourself through trial and error. While a lucky few get it right first time, most of us will have a few failed attempts along the way. But you're never going to get anywhere if you don't pay attention to past mistakes. If you burnt your cake last time (yes, we're still baking here. Bear with me, we're nearly done) and use exactly the same method this time, you're going to get exactly the same results.

So, before you start writing your profile and listing the qualities you're looking for in a partner, have a think about the ingredients your previous partners were missing and the aspects of your relationship that didn't work. It's all very well advertising for a snowboarding muso who's over six foot, but if he's selfish and arrogant like ex number one, or a doormat like ex number two, you're going to revisit the same old issues.

Be clear about what you really want this time and stick to your guns. If there are aspects of his profile or hints in his email that are reminiscent of failed relationships past, don't think you will be able to change this one. You won't. Happy baking!

Manage your expectations

What is it you really want to achieve from joining a dating site? Is it a bit of fun? A short-term fling? A FWB (friend with 'benefits')? A serious relationship? Marriage, 2.4 children, a Renault Espace and a second home on the Amalfi Coast? If it's the latter, you might want to go for the 12-month subscription deal. Don't forget we're talking about online dating here, not mail-order husbands. Sure, you're going to meet a lot of men, but if you're hoping to fast-track that fairytale ending and skip to the part where you go skipping down the aisle, you could be setting yourself up for a fall (well, if you will skip while wearing a wedding dress . . .).

Let me be a horrible warning #1:
'I've got a good feeling about this one'

As a hopeless romantic who 'falls in love' several times a day (on the train/in the supermarket queue/walking down the street/at traffic lights . . .) I thought all my Valentine's days had come at once when I first signed up to mysinglefriend.com a couple of years ago. I couldn't leave my laptop for more than five minutes without a potential new boyfriend popping up on my 'who likes me' page or in my inbox. One glimpse of a cool T-shirt or a beard on his profile picture and I'd be away with the fairies planning the décor of our first flat. This would be magnified tenfold if the hot picture was also accompanied with witty email banter. In fact I 'fell in love' over email about four times during that first month.

Before each date I'd wave goodbye to my flatmate with the optimistic cry, 'I've got a really good feeling about this one!' only to return a couple of hours later with cries of, 'Five foot ten, my arse! He was shorter standing up than he was sitting down!' or 'I spilled Guinness in his crotch when he tried to stick his tongue in my mouth' or 'He forgot his wallet!' . . . It wasn't until date

---

five that I was finally able to say, 'I was right! He was amazing!' But of course, date number five never called.

I know I'm painting a bleak picture here, but really I'm not trying to put you off. Don't get me wrong, I loved the excitement and drama of those first few dates and I've had plenty of amazing dates since. After all, I wouldn't be writing this book if I'd given up there and then. But I did learn pretty quickly that the higher your expectations, the bigger the disappointment when the chemistry is a no-show, come date time. Those highs and lows can get pretty exhausting after a while. So while it's good to maintain an optimistic and positive attitude, you probably don't want your mum wedding-hat shopping until . . . ooh, at least date three.

Reassess your 'tick-list'

I've always had a reputation for being way too fussy when it comes to men. It's not that I position myself at the top of the dating league table. I've never gone for model good looks, high-powered jobs or six-figure salaries. Quite the opposite in fact: Impoverished artist? Tick. A cavalier attitude to shaving? Tick. On the skinny side? Tick. Scruffy trainers? Tick. According to a more broad-minded friend, it was the 'sheer breadth and detail' of my boyfriend-criteria checklist that eventually drove all my regular cupids to hang up their bows in despair. So when I started online dating I decided it was time to be a bit more open-minded and step out of my comfort zone. And sure enough, some of the best dates I've ever been on have been with the men I've least expected.

Don't get me wrong, I'm not suggesting you scrap your standards and go out with every bloke who contacts you. Even now, I will not entertain a man who likes musicals or irons his underpants, even if he is the sweetest man on the planet and once built a house singlehandedly from scratch. All I'm suggesting is that you don't rule someone out based on the fact you don't like the fleece he's wearing in his third picture (he's up a mountain in Norway for heaven's sake – it's cold!).

Have a think back to all the guys you've ever fallen for. Did they really tick every single box? Were they all exactly the same height with the same hair colour, same job and same taste in footwear? Did the relationship ultimately end because he didn't wear the right shoes or because he was 5'10" instead of 6'2"? No probably not. The chances are it ended because your person-alities or your goals were different. Ultimately this is what you need to focus on, not the shallow stuff.

> ### But, but, but . . .your lame excuses busted!
>
> **Q:** *'I'm tempted to try online dating but none of my friends are doing it. I don't want to be the first. If they find out I'll never live it down.'*
>
> **A:** I didn't want to be the first out of all my mates to take the plunge with online dating either, but as most of them seemed to be happily coupled up I felt it was either resign myself to a lifetime of Saturday nights with *Family Fortunes* and family-sized bars of chocolate, or swallow my pride. I not only signed up, but in a bid to help remove the stigma from the whole thing I decided

to go public and wrote a column about my experience in *Cosmo*. The funny thing is, as soon as I did, dozens of single friends started creeping out of the online dating closet. It turned out half the *Cosmo* office were online, but nobody had wanted to be the first to admit it. And the numbers are creeping up every day. According to research, online dating is now officially the most popular way to find love in Britain so you certainly won't be the first; you might just be the first to admit it.

Q: 'I'm rubbish at emailing. My grammar is terrible and I find it hard to be myself in emails. I never know what to say.'

A: The idea of online dating is not to find yourself a new pen pal. You've got your 397 Facebook 'friends' for that. The point is to get yourself out on dates meeting people. In fact, if we spent less time glued to our keyboards and more time getting out and about meeting people we probably wouldn't need to turn to online dating in the first place. So stop fretting about the 'online' part and focus on the important bit: 'dating'. Don't worry about wowing him with your words. At this point he really just wants to establish that you have a few things in common and that you're not a crazed psycho likely to end up watching him from behind parked cars/boiling his bunny if things don't work out. He'll work out the rest later. Also, bear in mind that a lot of men hate emailing too so they'll probably be relieved if you want to take things offline sooner rather than later.

Q: 'I hate going on dates. I don't have the confidence. I get really nervous beforehand and i'm quite shy.'

A: The thing about dates is that *nobody* likes them. In fact, most people dread them. Even him. When he emails you and says he'd like to get to know you better over a drink, what he really means is he'd like to be five dates down the track with you when you've got through all the small talk, decided you actually quite like each other and have started sleeping together. So don't think for a second you're in this alone. While you're chucking clothes around your bedroom in a blind panic, trying to decide what to wear, he's going through exactly the same dread and anxiety as you ('T-shirt too scruffy? Shirt too formal?'/'Will she think I'm over-keen if I wear aftershave?'). But the great thing about dates is a) they're usually a lot less scary than you expect, b) even the bad ones are over in a flash and c) the more you go on, the easier they get.

Q: 'I'm quite fussy about men. I only really go for the cool muso types (preferably in a band). You don't get the really "cool" men on those sites.'

A: On the contrary, even the painfully trendy types who are 'way too cool' are doing it these days – they're just not telling their mates. A few months ago I met Paul*. He had the cool trainers, the music collection, the creative job . . . and most importantly he was good mates with one of my favourite bands (result!). I couldn't believe someone so cool could be found online. The problem was, neither could he. Every time one of his 'cool' mates asked us how we met he would jump in with, 'Out and about!' I got used to the lying, but it really began to chip away at my confidence when he was too ashamed to tell his friends I was a dating columnist and was writing a book about online dating. In the end, I realised being cool wasn't actually that cool at all and that I'd rather be with someone who liked me for who I was so I ditched him. He gave me a big spiel about how internet dating was for losers and he'd never do it again. So how amused was I to find him back on the site two weeks later under a new name? I guess the question you should be asking yourself is not whether the cool guys are on there but whether or not they're as cool as you think.

Ditch your preconceptions

Before you start fraternising with fellow daters you'll need to ditch any internet dating hang-ups you might have – or at least have the decency to keep them to yourself. After all, you're all in the same boat. If you go into this feeling ashamed and embarrassed, with the attitude that you're scraping the bottom of the barrel, people will pick up on your cynicism and be put off by your negative vibes.

You're not doing this because you're desperate. You're doing it because quite frankly you've got better things to do with your Saturday nights than trawling bars hoping to meet Prince Charming. You've got a life and a busy, exciting one at that.

Your Top 5 objections . . . overruled

Objection 1: It's too expensive.

Overruled: A month's subscription to the top sites costs about the same as a night out on the pull . . . except all the men are single and you don't get drunk losers falling all over you.

Objection 2: I'm too busy.

Overruled: Logging in for five minutes a day is all you need to browse the latest profiles and check your inbox and fans page . . . it beats reading what one of your friends had for breakfast on Facebook.

Objection 3: I've had a quick browse and don't like the look of the men.

Overruled: You only have to step into a bar/walk down the street/scan your office to see that real life ain't no Hollywood movie, but the gems are there when you look for them and you really can't tell from one snap-shot. Give them a chance.

Objection 4: My friend tried it and didn't meet anyone she liked.

Overruled: There are all kinds of reasons why things might not have worked out for your friend. Maybe it was the wrong timing or the wrong site. The only way to know whether it will work for you is to have a look for yourself. You wouldn't avoid going to a bar because one of your friends didn't pull in there, would you?

Objection 5: I don't have anything cool to say in my profile.

Overruled: What, you mean you haven't circum-navigated the globe in a recycled canoe to save polar bears from melting ice caps while reading the complete works of Shakespeare in Mandarin? Well, I'll let you into a little secret, neither has anyone else – everyone's just writing what they think people want to hear. The most popular girls' profiles are short, sweet . . . and a bit silly.

One step at a time

Remember this is just an internet dating site. It's meant to be a bit of fun – you're not signing up to the army. There is nothing to be afraid of because you're the one calling the shots. Nobody is going to force you to go on a date with anybody you don't want to. There are no rules about sleeping with someone before your sub-scription runs out. So take your time.

Most reputable sites will allow you to register and browse other people's profiles without paying a penny, so if you want to get a bit of an insight into who's out there, how it all works and which site works for you, without any commitment, register with a few different sites and see which one feels best. Think of it as sussing out the bar on a night out in a new town. Many sites will even allow you to create a profile and start adding people to your favourites for free, so this is a good way to dip your toe into the dating pool. If you like what you see, set up your profile for unlimited browsing. If you like the people responding to you and would like to start making contact, look at the package options. The longer you sign up for the better the deal, but don't feel forced into signing up for six months. A month may be all you want to begin with.

CHAPTER 2

Finding The Right Site For You

So many sites, so many men . . . so little time

You only have to type 'online dating sites' into a Google search to see proof that looking for love on the web is no longer a minority pursuit for the desperate and the deviant. The industry has exploded in the last couple of years and is positively booming right now, with hundreds of sites out there, boasting thousands of members and a promise to find your Prince Charming, whether it's a soul mate or a sugar daddy on your wish list. So, if you still reckon there is a stigma attached and that none of your mates would consider stooping so low as to sign up to a dating site, you might want to ask yourself how many of them are just not 'fessing up.

But whether you're proud to join the dating revolution or you just want to have a little dabble on the sly to see what all the fuss is about, the question remains, which site is the right one for you? The best value for money, the most advanced features, the greatest number of men, the

17

most likely to attract your 'type' . . . there are all manner of things to bear in mind when you're shopping for a new love life. Here's a lowdown of the best of the bunch (all prices were correct at the time of press, but check the websites for the latest offers).

My top rated . . .

cosmopolitan.co.uk

What's the big deal?
With over 35 years of advice on sex, relationships and dating under its belt, you'd be hard pushed to find a more trusted source to play cupid for you than Cosmo. When you're browsing the site, the profiles most suited to Cosmo readers are pulled to the front so you even get a helping hand to sort the young hotties from the 50-year-old stamp collectors. And the best bit? The cupids at Cosmo have had the genius idea of linking up the matchmakers at Men's Health Magazine – yes, that's right, home of the sexy six-pack hunks. Now if that's not a big deal, I don't know what is.

The talent
Er, super-fit Men's Health Magazine readers? Get your buff bodies here.

The features
Write your own dating diary and check out other users' diaries; plus find out if your future together is written in the stars with the horoscopes, birth date report, romantic profile report, and a sun, love and passion profile.

What's the deal?

You can browse profiles and upload you own profile and pictures for free. Becoming a subscriber allows you to do advanced searches to find men who fit your criteria and send and receive messages. The rate is:

£14.95/month

mysinglefriend.com

What's the big deal?

MSF has a special place in my heart because this is where my online adventures began a couple of years ago. The site has a slightly younger audience than many of the mainstream sites with the majority of daters ranging from early twenties to late thirties. One of its biggest selling points for many is that you don't have the cringe-factor of writing your own profile, the idea being that you get one of your mates to big you up instead.

The brainchild of property guru and TV presenter Sarah Beeney, MSF began with a few of Sarah's own single friends and has grown from word of mouth as their friends have invited their friends to join and their friends have invited theirs and so on. As a result, the site tends to attract like-minded types (great if you fit their demographic – see below) and the standard is fairly consistent.

The talent

Young, successful professionals, sporty and out-doorsy types, city-dwellers, creatives, the educated and ambitious, lookers (there are some seriously sexy men on here), a middle-class leaning.

The features

From heart-melting success stories to dating advice from experts, the blog is entertaining and useful.

What's the deal?

You can browse profiles, upload your own profile and add users to your favourites list for free. To become a subscriber, which allows you to do advanced searches to find men who fit your criteria and send and receive messages, the rates are:

£18 for 1 month
£27 for 2 months
£34 for 3 months

guardiansoulmates.co.uk

What's the big deal?

As the site that has brought me the most dating success, this is my personal site of choice – and not just because it has the highest quota of scruffy, bearded creative types. GS works harder than most sites to give you your money's worth. Unlike other sites where it's possible to get lost in the ether if you go for longer than 24 hours without logging on, GS offers numerous ways to ensure your profile is always easy to find. If you're not lucky enough to make it on to the Most Popular search list, he can find you in the Online Now, Who's Viewed Me, Recently Updated Profiles or Perfect Match sections. The more active you are, the more popular you'll become.

The talent

If you like your men educated, cultured, eco-conscious and well travelled, with an enquiring mind, a left-wing leaning and a plentiful supply of opinions, this is the site for you. Expect to find lots of creative/arty/muso types too. Think beards, cool trainers and geek-chic specs.

The features

By answering an extensive number of personal choice questions about yourself and your ideal match, the computer is able to 'match-make' you with the most compatible suitors. Having said that, I found most of my dates through the other search options. The Who's Viewed Me and Who's Online Now categories mean you not only get greater visibility on the site but you can browse the people you know are currently active and who have taken an interest in your profile. The downside of course is there is little privacy. This can make things a little tricky once you start multi-dating!

What's the deal?

You can browse other members' profiles, upload your own, add users to your favourites list, read email messages and respond to messages using a range of default one-liners, all for free. To become a subscriber, which allows you to do advanced searches to find men who fit your criteria and send and receive messages, the rates are:

£24.95 for 1 month
£17.95/month for 3 months
£12.95/month for 6 months

21

datingdirect.co.uk and uk.match.com

What's the big deal?
Match and Dating Direct are the daddies of the dating world when it comes to their sheer size and popularity. Offering the greatest number of singles online to choose from, they're probably a safe bet if your taste in men isn't too specific or quirky. Probably the most established dating site around, Match prides itself on helping you to find your most compatible match with its extensive search function. With over 5 million UK members, Dating Direct is number one for choice – and if you can't find someone out of that lot within six months there's even a money-back guarantee.

The talent
Quantity and diversity is the major selling point for these mainstream sites. From brickies to brain surgeons, Match and Dating Direct offer a complete cross section covering every walk of life.

The features
The search function on Match is second to none and includes a free personality test to ensure you get to see the men who tick the most boxes in your potential-boyfriend criteria tick list (and let's face it, we've all got one). Dating Direct, on the other hand, prides itself on its advanced tools, including instant chat and webcam facilities. DD will also send you daily email updates of potential matches.

What's the deal?

Both Match and Dating Direct allow you to register, browse profiles and upload your own profile for free. For full membership, which allows you to email other users, the rates are:

	Match	Dating Direct
1 month	£22.80	£22.80
3 months	£15.22/month	£14.99/month
6 months	£10.88/month	£9.99/month

10 of the best of the rest . . .
1. Plentyoffish.com
2. Friendfinder.com
3. Datetheuk.com
4. Dating.telegraph.co.uk
5. Friendsreuniteddating.com
6. Loopylove
7. Girlsdateforfree
8. Person.com
9. Mate1.com
10. Smooch.com

If you're broke . . . Flirtbox.co.uk

This is a completely free dating site with no subscriber fee so you can communicate with other users and save your pennies for those all-important dates.

If you're embarrassed about online dating . . . Facebook SpeedDate

According to numerous surveys, social networks are rapidly becoming the most popular way to find love. If nobody on your friends list is floating your boat, what's the harm in adding a little dating application? It's not like proper online dating, right?

If you're Jewish . . . jdate.com

The most popular online Jewish dating community, this has hundreds of thousands of members worldwide to help Jewish singles to find like-minded souls in their area.

If you're gay . . . gaydar.co.uk

Almost all dating sites enable you to search for same-sex partners, but this specialist site boasts the largest number of gay personals on the web.

If you're a bookworm . . . penguinmatch.com

Whoever said book clubs were the preserve of middle-aged cross-stitching women? Find yourself a like-minded book *lover* here.

If you're a single parent . . . DatingforParents.com

This is an established site with years of experience in helping to match single parents with dates who also have children or with people who are happy to meet someone who already has a family.

If you're a workaholic . . . lunchdate.com

If too much overtime means you can't find a window free for finding romance, fret not. Lunchdate.com is geared to helping you find love in your lunch hour.

If you're a gold digger . . . sugardaddie.com

If you're the kind of young lady who isn't too proud to use a man for his wallet, this site is full of minted men who are willing to buy their love.

If you're up for fun . . . smartdatinguk.com

Describing itself as a 'one-stop singles shop' this site covers a whole range of dating events and ideas from skiing and mountain bike holidays to wine tasting and movie events.

Choosing a site: DOs and DON'Ts

DO: Take your time window-shopping

Imagine you've decided to go shopping for a sexy new bag. I'm not talking about the kind you take on two nights out before the lining starts to rip and the handle breaks. Or the sort that's so trendy it's already surrendered its 'it' status to the 'next big thing' by the time the weekend arrives. I'm talking about a keeper. I mean the kind of bag that's going to carry you through (well, you're going to carry it through) the next few seasons and beyond. The kind your daughter will find in the back of your wardrobe in three decades time and covet because it's 'so vintage cool'. Yes, that kind of bag. Okay, now you wouldn't walk into the first shop, pick up the first bag you see, hand over your hard-earned cash and expect to live happily ever after with it, would you? Well, obviously, your bag is far more important than any man but if you want a good one, he is worth a little shopping around for, surely. There are so many sites out there. Make the most of the choice on offer.

DON'T: Sign up without a recommendation

Whether your best friend swears by it, all the girls at work are on there, it's recommended in this book or you've read about it in the paper or in a magazine article, always go for a site that has received some kind of recommendation from a trusted source. Apart from upping your chances of having a more satisfying experience, when it comes to forming relationships online you can never be too careful about your security and safety. From handing over your credit card details to arranging to hook up with virtual strangers, you are putting your trust in the hands of the site, so use your common sense. If you have any doubts about any of the members on the site or anything unusual during the credit card payment process, report it to the site moderators immediately and in the latter case, your bank, too.

DO: Spend wisely

Dating can be a pricey business. What with the outfits, the bar tabs and the cab fares home, you need every penny you can lay your manicured mitts on. So the last thing you need is to be throwing your cash away on badly planned subscription choices. If you're on a tight budget beware of 'false economy' traps. Cheapest doesn't necessarily mean the best value. It might only be £5 a month, but if it has only got ten members or they're not your kind of men, it's £5 down the drain. The longer you sign up for the cheaper it works out per month, so if you like to take things slowly it's worth considering a three or six month deal. On the other hand if you're not sure whether online dating is for you, a one-month trial makes more sense. Another thing to bear in mind is whether you're going to be around to make the most of your subscription. You'd be surprised how many people sign up before a two-week holiday.

DON'T: Forget to read the small print

Processing your credit card payment can be frustrating enough as it is, without having to plough through all those boring terms and conditions. Especially when that gorgeous bloke has just emailed you and you have some urgent flirting to get on with. Whoever reads those things, anyway? Well, not me, until I joined up with a site and failed to notice that they renew your subscription automatically unless you specify otherwise. Many sites do this to kindly save their members the job of thinking about it each month (in other words, to take advantage of those dumb asses who can't be bothered to read the small print). It's always worth taking five minutes out to read everything thoroughly, including the Frequently Asked Questions sections, before you make any financial commitments. You have no rights once you've ticked that box to say you agree to their terms.

DO: Give it a chance

If you log on expecting your screen to be crammed with more gorgeous specimens than you'd find in a *Cosmo* Centrefold Calendar, you're going to be bitterly disappointed. Just as you would be if you walked into a bar expecting the room to be crammed with more gorgeous specimens than you'd find at a *Cosmo* Centrefold Calendar Christmas party; unless you were actually walking into the *Cosmo* Centrefold Calendar Christmas party.

Just as online dating sites aren't full of freaks and geeks, nor are they full of perfect men. Unfortunately, technology hasn't yet progressed to the point where sites can create the men for you. Mark my words, when it has I will be writing the book on that one, too. Sadly, at this stage they just offer a random cross section of real-life human beings, which means you're unlikely to find The Man of your Dreams in the first five minutes. Patience, my friend.

DON'T: Give up after one site

If you went into a clothes shop to find a new outfit but couldn't find anything that suited you, would you:

a) Go straight home and vow never to set foot in another clothes shop again in the hope that a new way of accumulating clothes would be invented before all yours become thread-bare then fall apart and you had to walk around naked?

b) Try the clothes shop next door to see if there's anything in there, and if that doesn't work out, try the next one and so on until you have found the perfect outfit that makes you look pretty damn sexy, even if you say so yourself?

Just as some of us might swear by Topshop, while others have a wardrobe filled almost entirely with Warehouse, the site that works for one person isn't necessarily going to work for the next, so you need to shop around until you find your ideal match.

In your words . . .

'They say chemistry has nothing to do with ticking boxes but plenty of us seems to have an uncanny knack of seeking out compatible matches with its online "chemistry test". I had spent months dating Mr Wrongs on other sites then registered on here and found myself choosing between three lovely men within three weeks.' Adriana, 24, Manchester

'I like my men to be more than just a pretty face – and a little bit more mature than the usual laddish types that try to chat you up in bars. I met lots of lovely guys on the Telegraph dating site. The main difference being that they actually had interesting things to talk about. The last one I met married me!' Catherine, 27, Surrey

'I'd tried a couple of sites with little success but then a friend recommended match.com. There just seemed to be so much more choice. I loved the fact you get matched up with like-minded people too so you're not wasting too much time trawling through profiles of men you have nothing in common with.' Dawn, 23, Cheshire

'mysinglefriend was an absolute godsend. I don't think I would ever have joined a dating site if I'd had to write my own profile. It didn't feel half as bad having my friend sing my praises. She did a brilliant sales pitch too – I'm totally loved up with a guy I met three months ago. He said it was my profile that did it. I doubt we'd be together if I'd written it!' Julie, 29, Isle of Wight

CHAPTER 3
The Write Impression

Help! Profile panic

Now for the moment you've all been dreading – creating your profile! Unless you have a Paris Hilton-sized ego, telling the world how brilliant you are probably comes about as naturally as telling your best mate that her bum looks big in that. In fact, many of us seem to be far more comfortable pointing out our flaws than our fabulousness. But remember this is your opportunity to grab the attention of thousands of sexy, single, love-hungry men so now is not the time to be hiding your light under a bushel. Here's how to beat that profile paranoia . . .

It's 'blonde-moment' proof

'But creating the perfect profile is so much pressure!' I hear you collectively sigh. To that, I say it's a lot less pressure than trying to impress a guy face to face in a bar or at the bus stop. If only real life came with Photoshop, spell-check and a delete key, we'd all be laughing . . . and probably loved up right now.

Let me be a horrible warning #2: Never go out in furry slippers

Take the morning I bumped into Fit Bloke From Downstairs Flat in the corner shop last summer. Hungover as hell and white as a sheet, with red-wine-stained lips and Russell Brand hair, I looked like I was on my way home from a Halloween party. As I turned the corner to join the check-out queue, juggling my wares (Paracetemol, can of Coke, king-sized Mars Bar, box of tampons) I slipped on an unidentified spillage and went flying straight into FBFDF, dropping everything at his feet. For a second, time froze, then to my relief I saw a smile spread across his face as he looked down. All was not lost. Until I realised why he was grinning. I think the words were, 'Nice slippers'.

You see, with online dating there is no fear of a bad hair day/spinach in the teeth/foot in mouth moment because you've got all the time you want to prepare yourself for that fateful second he claps eyes on you. Result!

But before you start penning your 'Pick me, I'm amazing!' campaign, you will most likely need to set up a username and password and plough through a gazillion multiple-choice questions about yourself and your ideal match. Nobody said the path to true love was going to be easy.

What's in a name?

Most sites will ask you to create a username. When it comes to his perfect-girlfriend-criteria-tick-list, it's unlikely that 'good username' figures in his top 100. But then again, after a quick scan of your profile picture, this is probably the first thing he's going to notice. So wouldn't it be great if you could make a difference with yours?

There are three avenues you could take with this. I highly recommend the latter:

1. The bad

A common mistake is trying too hard to sound sexy and instead just sounding like the kind of girl who frequents sex chat rooms. Call yourself sexy_minx69 and you may as well cut to the chase and dress up as a dominatrix for your profile shot. Sure, you'll get plenty of attention, but unless it's one night with Heavy Breathing Harold you're after, it's unlikely to be the kind of attention you're looking for.

2. The boring

We've all been there. You're trying to set up a Yahoo/Hotmail/Google account with your name on it. But of course your name has already gone, as has your name followed by 1, 2, 3, 4, 156 . . . So you try following it with the year you were born. D'oh, that's gone too. How about putting _ between your first and last name? Oh no, too late! Before you know it you're georgia_barlow_321_74_london@blah, blah, blah. Not exactly catchy is it? The upshot is, if you end up with some convoluted codename with numbers all over it you might just miss out to the girl with the cool name next to yours.

3. The babe

If in doubt, go for something a bit quirky or tongue-in-cheek. That way he instantly knows you have a GSOH. While you don't want to sound too provocative and overtly sexual there's nothing wrong with being a bit cheeky and flirtatious. One that I noticed recently was 'Breakfastinbed'. Okay, so it makes a bedroom reference, but if anything it conjures up images of a romantic lazy Sunday morning snuggled up under the duvet. What man could resist that? Had it been accompanied with a saucy bed shot it would have seemed a bit too obvious but the picture was of a cute girl outdoors grinning to camera in a woolly hat. This girl gave me serious profile envy and I was not surprised to see her head straight to the Most Popular list on Guardian Soulmates.

Get-yourself-noticed names: *cakeandwine* (cute); *MisDmin*a (cheeky); *Butter_wouldn't_melt* (minx)

Talking of which, if you get stuck it's always an idea to check out the competition – particularly the most popular profiles – for inspiration. But no name nicking. You are a one-off original, right?

Ticking boxes

In a bid to play cupid and pair you up with supposedly compatible matches, most sites require that you fill out a number of multiple-choice questions about yourself as well as what you're looking for in a partner. Because of course love is all about ticking boxes, nothing to do with chemistry and feelings, right? Okay so not even Bill Gates could devise a computer programme to predict whether or not you're going to fancy the pants off someone. In fact, internet dating demonstrates like nothing else that the man who ticks the most boxes isn't necessarily going to be the one who floats your boat when you meet him in the flesh (and vice versa, I'm afraid).

But before you despair of this time-consuming non-sense, just think of the time it could save you in the long run. This is a brilliant opportunity to spot the deal-breakers before you even meet. There's nothing worse than meeting a guy in a bar, getting yourself whipped up into a complete frenzy of excitement and hope, only to discover on date four (by which point you're already thinking honeymoon destinations and baby names) that he is only looking for a casual fling and hates kids.

Be honest: When filling out the questions about yourself, be completely honest about the stuff that's set in stone. It's one thing to tick 'eats healthily' when you've just polished off a KFC, but it's another to say you're 28 when you're actually 35. You can start your healthy regime tomorrow but when are you going to be 28 again? Rule of thumb: Don't give any false answers that could bite you on the bum when you meet. Just think how you would react if the shoe was on the other foot.

Real-life case study

'I was pretty excited about meeting Jon. On his profile, he claimed to be a 24-year-old, sporty chocolate salesman (too good to be true right?). His picture wasn't my usual type, but he seemed quite funny on his emails and so I put my doubts to one side and agreed to go on a date with him – after all that is the point. I suggested we meet on a Sunday lunchtime for a walk but he insisted we go for a drink one evening, so we planned to meet in West London one Thursday night.

Anyway, I arrived a little early in order to scope out the scene first. I saw this substantially older man arrive and head to the area where we had agreed to meet. He took out his phone, and shortly after I received a text saying he was there. I was horrified – the man who had turned up was quite clearly a lot older than he had said online – late 30s at best, was losing his hair, had more around the middle than your average sporty Aussie (probably all the chocolate) and looked exceedingly shifty.

I know this is really bad but I couldn't go through with it. I sent him a text to say that I'd been held up at work and was really sorry and promptly broke into a run in the other direction. I tried to protect his feelings and didn't mention that it was a case of see and run, but he sent me a really aggressive message the next day saying that if I wasn't prepared to go on dates I should take myself off the site – he had a point but I thought that was a little harsh seeing how sometimes people DO get held up at work and I might have been about to suggest a rain check. But there we go. I took myself off the site the next day!' Sarah, 25, London

Be selective: If in any doubt about an answer, leave it out. Most sites will have a blank or 'ask me later' option. Don't feel obliged to reveal your every whim and foible. You're a potential new girlfriend, not a second-hand car. Some of this has to be left to the hand of fate surely.

Be open-minded: Cut the guys some slack when filling in the questions about your ideal match. In fact, forget the phrase 'ideal match'. Understand what your deal breakers are (10 years too young, smoker, lives 500 miles away . . .) and be clear about those, but try not to be too restrictive with the shallow stuff. Does height really matter? Personally, I have always had a thing for boys who are 6'3" and over but when I thought about all the sexy men I've ever known or lusted after under 5'11", I realised that by filtering out Mr Small I could be missing out on something big, so I set my stall out at 5'8" and above (after all a girl needs to be able to wear four-inch heels and still feel like a girl). The upshot is, the wider you cast your net the greater your chance of catching Mr Right.

Crash course in confidence

If you haven't developed a nasty case of RSI by now from clicking your way through all those questions, it's time for the tricky bit – your sales pitch. If, like me, you find it much easier to put yourself down than big yourself up, you may have stumbled upon the key to why you're still single. After all, if you don't rate yourself how is anyone else supposed to?

If you're feeling good about yourself when you write your profile, it will really shine through and make you more man-magnetic. So as a self-esteem boosting exercise, start by making a list of all your good points. This could be anything from being a great listener or calm in a crisis to being eco-conscious or baking mean brownies. The most important thing to remember is that this list is for your eyes only. This isn't going public so don't let modesty hold you back. Don't be afraid to throw in the shallow stuff, either. If secretly you know you have nice eyes and a perky bum, write it down. I won't tell anyone.

Confidence kicked to the curb by your last relationship? Then it's time to phone a friend. When you're suffering from a spot of self-loathing you can't beat a few kind words of encouragement from your nearest and dearest. Most of us have at least one person we can rely on to make us feel ten feet tall when we're feeling like crap. Give that friend a call and ask her to make a list of all the reasons she thinks you're a top mate. This will remind you that, whatever might have gone wrong with your last relationship, you really are a chick worth hanging out with. You'll probably discover brilliant new things about yourself you weren't even aware of.

10 steps to a magnetic profile

Ready now, hot stuff? Then it's time to start penning your personal sales pitch. Don't worry you don't need to be an ace saleswoman or a prolific writer. Just follow these common-sense guidelines and you'll get more male attention than the FA Cup final.

1. Be honest . . .

Telling porkies on your profile is a bit like lying on your CV. You know it could improve your chances, but you'll look like a complete loser if you get sprung. Claiming you're an ace snowboarder or mountain biker might help you score a date with sexy Mr Extreme. But faking it online is the easy bit – faking it on top of a mountain, come date three, is a bit trickier.

As a (suspiciously mud-free) mountain bike owner with a penchant for fit, outdoorsy types with rock-hard thighs, I chose the honest route:

'If you're willing to spend Saturday afternoon lingering around an art gallery with me (even when you don't like the artist) I'll agree to come mountain biking in the rain on Sunday, but just don't complain if I'm a bit rubbish.'

This says, 'I'm happy to admit I'm not perfect but I'm willing to give things a go.' And it worked – an hour later I got an email from a sexy mountain biker. And yes, his thighs were rock hard.

You see most of the guys out there are not searching for an Olympic athlete/four-star Michelin cook/best-selling novelist/Turner-prize winning artist (delete as applicable). They just want a like-minded soul with a few shared interests. Does it matter if she's imperfect? No. Does it matter if she's untrustworthy? Hell, yeah.

2. . . . Really honest

And by dishonesty, I include anything that's deliberately misleading like the campus caretaker who was 'working in academia', the one-time *Emmerdale* extra claiming to be an 'actor' and the McDonald's burger-flipper who was a 'head chef in well-known successful restaurant' (I kid ye not). Honestly, if Trading Standards ever got involved in online dating they'd have a field day.

The point is it doesn't matter whether you're a barrister or a barista as long as you're yourself so, as with the tick box section, avoid saying anything on your profile that could lead to an embarrassing moment on the date.

If you're not particularly proud of your current job and would rather be judged on your personality than what you do for a living, keep things vague or leave it out entirely. You don't honestly think that I announced on my profile that I was writing a book about online dating, do you? I would have been about as popular as Heather Mills at a Beatles convention.

Instead, I just said I was a writer. If anyone asked me the details, I didn't lie, I just breezily quipped, 'Oh, I'm working on a book about boys and dating for *Cosmo*. But don't worry, you're not about to end up on Waterstone's bookshelf.' I left it up to them whether to trust me or run a mile.

3. Woah, not that honest!

Of course, there's honest and then there's TMI. I mean how often do you hear the phrase TLI (too little information)? Exactly. Let's face it, we all have our moods, moments and off days. That's taken as a given. But there's no need to go advertising them at this stage. It's better to retain an air of mystery for as long as possible. Give him a chance to finish constructing that pedestal for you while he's still wearing his rose-stinted spectacles. You've got plenty of time to fall off it later (in my case, around month four after one too many glasses of red wine).

The aim of the game here is not to convince him you're perfect as that would be downright intimidating. A little bit of self-deprecation can be very attractive but just make sure you're selective about the flaws and foibles you reveal.

These girls have used their imperfections to their advantage to sound funny and endearing:

'I love experimenting in the kitchen, but don't ask my friends about the exploding pie incident.'

'I love Sunday mornings with a coffee and the papers. But if I'm really honest I usually only get round to reading the magazine bits. I do recycle though!'

'I'm into loads of stuff, a lot of which I'm quite crap at: Singing in the shower (crap); Scrabble (not so crap); painting (quite crap); cooking (pretty good); cryptic crosswords (crap); kissing (brilliant!).'

'I'd like a man who can catch spiders. I am yet to meet a spider that is more scared of me than I am of it.'

'I like putting on my walking boots and heading for the mountains, looking up at them in wonder for a bit, then marching straight to the nearest cosy pub.'

'I'm possibly one of the clumsiest people in the world and do many, many stupid things (I should

really write a book on it) and I never make sense, but if you can put up with that I'm actually quite nice.'

These girls, on the other hand, have given a frightening insight into life after the honeymoon period – and it ain't pretty. Definitely TMI:

'I'm generally quite laid back . . . apart from when I've got PMT. Then my mood swings make Naomi Campbell look as chilled as a Zen Buddhist. You've been warned.' (read: psycho)

'I've recently emerged from the other side of a messy break-up and am still feeling quite raw and bruised so please be gentle with me.' (read: issues)

'I'm pretty stubborn in arguments. That's probably because I'm usually right.' (read: ball breaker)

'My friends call me The Diva because I've been known to throw a tantrum when I don't get my own way. I think it's the only child in me. But if you indulge my inner princess I'm sure we'll get along just fine.' (read: high maintenance)

4. Avoid clichés

Picture the scene: You leave the house for a night out feeling pretty damn hot. You have one last check in the mirror. Rocking dress? Tick. Sexy hair? Tick. Smoulder-ing make-up? Tick. You've got a feeling tonight could be your lucky night . . . Until you walk into the bar where you are greeted by a sea of girls in identical black dresses, with poker-straight hair and smouldering make-up (yes, it's like a scene from *Hollyoaks*). Then just as you thought you couldn't get any more invisible a girl walks in wearing a bright red dress . . . No prizes for guessing who gets the most male attention.

My point is that if you're offering the same proposition as every other girl on the site, what's his incentive to click on you? If yours is the tenth profile he's read that day that says you're 'bubbly, ambitious and don't take yourself too seriously' he's going to sail straight past you.

So forget all the obvious generic stuff that applies to every other girl on the planet and think about your USPs (unique selling points). What is it that makes you different and interesting? What can you tell him that's going to get his attention?

Even something silly like your spoon-balancing party trick will help you to be noticed and remembered. Having said that, don't start being too flipped out: Think 'quirky' not 'weird'.

WARNING: These clichés could seriously damage your chances

I've spent months browsing profiles to suss out the most over-used lines so you don't have to.

'I'm equally at home partying the night away or curled up on the sofa with a DVD . . . "

Yes, yes you're equally at home when you're at home

42

and when you're not at home. I think it's safe to say, with the exception of a few extremists (hermits and hardcore ravers) that most of us like staying in sometimes and going out sometimes.

'My friends and family are very important to me.'

Have you ever met anyone whose friends are *not* important to them? Surely this goes without saying like 'I am a human being', or 'Breathing is important to me'.

'I'm new to this online dating lark . . .'

Oh, well if you're new, that makes you okay then. I mean it would be really sad if you'd been stuck on here for months, wouldn't it? Oh, hang on I've been on here for months. Are you saying I'm sad?

'Well, what can I say? . . .'

What the hell do I know? I've just spent a week agonising over my own profile and I've known myself for 34 years. How about something relevant? Interesting? Witty? Just get to the point, will you?

'I love the hustle and bustle of the city but also love to escape to the country . . .'

I don't think I've ever heard anyone under the age of 60 talking about enjoying the 'hustle and bustle of the city' down the pub? So why everyone insists on using these terrible phrases online, I'll never know.

'I'd like to meet a man who's honest, kind, caring . . .

No? Really? Well, join the queue love because that's the kind of man every woman on the planet would like to meet.

'I'm looking for someone who's prepared to lie about how we met'

I laughed the first time I read this line but please, enough already! The joke is over. Take the time to think of something original.

5. If in doubt, make a random list

This is not a writing competition. It's about getting your point across in as few words as possible before he moves on to the next profile. So forget the fluff and the flowery language and cut to the chase. If in doubt, go with a list stuff that reveals a bit about who you are.

The key is to keep the list interesting, relevant and a little bit random. Don't take it too seriously and don't be too generic. Throw in a few quirky little foibles that will make him smile and that he won't have read before as well as a few favourites such as books/places/films you love.

A good list (this gives a little snapshot of who she is):

I like: Hummus, kissing, Bob Dylan, laughing until I nearly wee, Lost in Translation, kissing, sparkly things, Revels in the cinema ('ooh, which one will it be next?'), positive people, a pint of Guinness on a Sunday afternoon, surprise visits to friends on my bike, back-to-back comedy DVD sessions, Magnus Mills books, Masterchef, David Hockney, dancing in people's living rooms after the pub . . . did I say kissing?

I don't like: Litter droppers, coffee flavoured Revels, people asking me questions before my morning coffee, laughing when I'm not supposed to (but I just can't help it).

A bad list (this says nothing unique. Why should anyone bother to get to know her?):

I like: travel, reading, keeping fit, films, galleries, open-mindedness, walks by the beach.

I don't like: moody people, grey skies, waiting in queues.

6. Don't diss online dating

Do you really need me to explain the glaring error? You would be amazed at how many people use the first 50 words of their profile to excuse the fact they're actually stooping so low as to be looking for love online. If you want to insult every single person who reads your profile – and yourself – in one fell swoop, then this is the way to go. Because, hello? Every single person who reads your profile is, um, online dating and *you* are, um, online dating. So let's just get over that fact and get on with it, shall we?

Nobody is going to cast you aside based on the fact you're on the site, are they? Then they'd have to ignore everyone on the site and that would be a massive waste of joining a dating site really, wouldn't it? And a bit weird. But they might overlook you because a) by suggesting you're above this online lark you sound arrogant b) you sound way too negative and cynical c) you're suggesting that only desperados online date and therefore you must think they're a desperado or d) they're so bored of reading the same old 'I'm not used to this . . . ' line they've already moved onto the next profile.

So let's scrap the embarrassed introduction, ditch the negativity and dive straight in with a brilliant reason why someone should take you out on a date.

7. Don't try too hard

While the aim of the game is to promote yourself and let him know what a great catch you are, don't be too obvious. If you try too hard to impress, you will come across as either arrogant or as someone insecure trying to sound cool – which of course is a one-way ticket to *un*cool.

Listing your entire CD and DVD collection in an attempt to impress musos and film buffs, for instance, will be painfully obvious. Showing off about the number of bands you've heard of/films you've seen should not really continue a moment after your 15th birthday.

Likewise, avoid listing every country you've ever visited, or reeling off a lifetime's worth of sporting achievements. You're far better saving a few surprises to drop in gradually as he gets to know you. There is nothing sexier than a woman who is modest about her fabulousness.

8. Make him laugh

It's all very well claiming to have your mates in stitches with your witty one-liners but if your profile is as sober as a church sermon, it's not going to wash. The best way to show a guy you're a bit of a giggle is to throw in a few funnies so he can see for himself.

We're not talking 'what did the nun say to the actor?' gags. Anyone can repeat a joke. Personal anecdotes will say much more about you. Don't be shy about throwing in an embarrassing story either. This is a good way to show you don't take yourself too seriously.

Be aware that irony doesn't always come across the way its intended without tone of voice to carry it. It's likely to sound as though you're being sarcastic, or worse, deadly serious.

If you have an absurd off-the-wall sense of humour and reflect this in your profile you might find that you get fewer hits as you'll only appeal to a niche market (absurd off-the-wall men), but that's probably not a bad thing. It's a great way to seek out like-minded souls.

'I am obscenely rich. Really. And I love to spend my money on whoever I'm dating. I will literally throw money at you on a regular basis for no reason at all. My last date bought himself a house in Mayfair recently with the suitcases of cash I gave him at the end of our evening.' Megan, 23, Berks

9. Say what you're looking for

No matter how specific you are with your requirements, nothing will stop you from being bombarded with emails from Mr Wrong. It's painfully apparent that a lot of men don't even bother to read the profiles and just randomly click on anyone they like the look of. But saying a few words about the kind of man you're looking for could certainly help you to catch the eye of a few potential Mr Rights.

Again, be specific. We're all looking for someone kind, considerate, loyal, caring and gorgeous, so focus on some of the little traits and foibles you're drawn towards.

Vague: *'If you don't take yourself too seriously, you have a job/life and a good group of friends then you might be onto a winner...'*

Boring: *'My ideal match would be intelligent, funny, good natured and adventurous! I don't believe in perfection but generally decent human characteristics are a must!'*

Cute: *'If you have a creative leaning, like talking until dawn, are not averse to a spot of exercise, warn before farting, like fish and chips, own a kite and love finding cheap second-hand records for under a pound, click here.'*

Tongue-in-cheek: *'I'm holding out for a man who can crack walnuts with one (bare) hand and change the oil in my car with the other, whilst waiting for the organic bread he just made to bake in the clay oven he built . . . Anyone? . . .'*

10. Be positive

Finally, be happy! A positive profile is the written equivalent of a radiant smile in your profile shot. There's no harm in throwing in a few things that you don't like, but remember to focus on the good stuff. If you start reeling off a big list of personal gripes and dislikes you're not exactly painting yourself as the ideal partner for a fun night out. Having a slightly dark and cynical sense of humour is one thing but moaning and whinging is about as attractive as bad breath. He's looking for someone to share good times with, a ray of sunshine in his life, not a harbinger of doom to rain on his parade.

A quick lesson in spelling and grammar

Okay, this isn't an English exam and admittedly, a lot of guys won't a) notice or b) care but many of the guys I spoke to said poor grammar and 2 MUCH OF DIS NONSENSE (LOL)!!! Can be a real turn-off. Here are some of the most common trouble spots.

Spelling: Two words: Spell check. If possible get a wordy friend to check what you've written, too. Bad spelling says you couldn't be bothered to make an effort.

Exclamation marks: Don't do this!!!!! I know you're enthusiastic but there's enthusiastic and then there's slightly deranged. To avoid coming across like a hyperactive child, cut the exclamation marks out altogether. Calm down. You're super-chilled and laid back, right?

Capitals: WRITING EVERYTHING IN CAPITAL LETTERS is the grammatical equivalent of shouting down your mobile in a quiet intimate restaurant. To put emphasis on a word without coming across like a loudmouth, write it in italics.

Paragraphs: Writing a profile without breaking it up into paragraphs is the equivalent of arriving on a date and wittering on for the first 20 minutes without drawing breath. If you want him to make it to the end, break it up after every couple of sentences.

Apostrophes: Use an apostrophe a) when you're saying something belongs to someone (Samantha's bag). If it belongs to more than one stick the apostrophe at the end (the girls' bags). The exception to this is when something belongs to it, or her (its, hers). The other use for an apostrophe is to represent missing letters when you're joining two words up ('she'll' as in she will or 'I've' as in I have, and 'it's' as in it is).

Their, there, they're: Always use 'there' except when you mean belonging to ('their shoes') or they are ('they're').

Still suffering from profile panic?
Try mysinglefriend.com

If you're still drawing a blank on the profile-writing front, it might be time to change tactics and phone a friend. For this reason, many people gravitate towards mysinglefriend.com (see p. 18) where the idea is to have someone else write your glowing report. The great thing about this is that you get a rave review without having to blow your own trumpet. Also, your friends will probably pick up on the little things that make you fab that you weren't even aware of. All you have to do is write a couple of sentences in response to their comments.

PS Here's a sneak peek at the profile I wrote . . .

Do you like getting lost in new places? Good, because I have a heightened sense of adventure and an appalling sense of direction.

I've recently fallen in love with London again having spent the last few months in Barcelona so I'm in the mood for playing out. Gigs, galleries, cinema, bicycle adventures and the like.

I like playing in, too. In the kitchen. But cooking is less fun for one.

I like writing and conversations that go off on a tangent and take you into the wee small hours. I like observing the absurdities of the everyday and laughing very hard.

I like thought-provoking, stunning films that are always big on character and mood, sometimes low on plot* but make you want to leg it to the nearest pub to talk about them on the way home.

I think music is the food of love. I think food is the food of love, too...hmm, and laughter. Good spelling kind of does it for me too, come to think of it.

*I can't deny this is largely because I am not very good with complex plots. I forget to concen . . .

My ideal match . . .

. . . can make me laugh at 7 on a Monday morning.

. . . usually has a little project on the go and gets all passionate when he talks about it.

. . . gives me the occasional kiss on the neck when I'm cooking/reading/working.

. . . surprises me with new places to go and things to see – like an obscure little gig in a kooky venue.

. . . has opinions and cares about mine too.

. . . is a top mate.

. . . will come with me to see an exhibition even if he isn't that keen on the artist (in return I'll agree to go mountain biking in the rain – just don't complain if I'm a bit rubbish).

. . . will be my 'Orange-Wednesday-two-for-the-price-of-one' cinema partner.

. . . is a good kisser.

Beard = bonus.

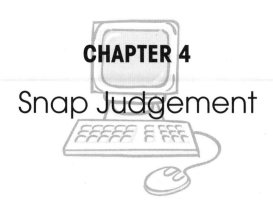

CHAPTER 4

Snap Judgement

We all know that your photo is the bit he's *really* interested in. Of course, ideally, he'd like that to be backed up with some solid evidence in your profile that you're no bimbo/bitch/ bunny-boiler, but ultimately if he doesn't like your picture in the first instance there's a chance he won't even get as far as reading about your impressive extreme sports accolades and third world charity work. After all, he won't have time to read every profile out there, so it makes sense he'll start with the ones with attractive pictures.

This may sound horribly shallow, but if we're honest, we all do it – whether we're browsing profiles or casually scanning a bar. We are animals after all and there is no denying the fact that physical attraction is key when it comes to sexual chemistry.

So, ready for your close-up?

But don't worry, the good news is an attractive picture has nothing to do with model good looks. In fact, during my research (a brilliant excuse to chat to hundreds of single men) I discovered that most guys prefer approachable girls-next-door with winning smiles to pouting wannabe supermodels. So, before you get yourself airbrushed to within an inch of your life, or worse, book yourself into a professional photography studio, check out these tips on how to look picture perfect (without the soft-focus lens).

10 steps to a winning pic

1. Does it look like you? There's no point having a picture up there if it's impossible to see what you look like. Your main shot should ideally be a close-up of your head and shoulders with your face to camera. If it's blurry, you're turned away, wearing a ski hat and goggles or you're a tiny distant figure on top of an elephant (you can show off about your travels on your extra shots), he's going to be none the wiser. This goes for those arty black and white shadowy shots, too. It might do wonders for your cheekbones but he's just going to wonder what you're hiding behind those shadows.

2. Think about the outfit: Avoid anything too fussy that will distract from your face. Your eyes and smile will say a lot more about you than your new bling-tastic necklace. Try to choose a photo that reflects your own personal style. If you're a grungy indie chick, that shot of you in a bridesmaid's meringue dress is probably not going to bag you a band boy. If in doubt, go for a snap of you in your favourite Friday-night outfit. By the way, a word of warning: Beware of strapless tops. If it's cropped in you will look naked. It's one way to get attention but will it really be the kind of attention you want?

3. What's behind you? Check for any classic background blunders like 'plant growing out of head' syndrome or 'person making rabbit ears behind you' (believe it or not, there are plenty of those out there). Busy backgrounds will distract from the main attraction (you) so if in doubt, keep it simple, but bonus points if you can find a backdrop that reflects your personality whether it be a crisp autumn day in the country, at the top of a piste, on a sunny beach or having a good old boogie at a gig. (Don't forget the flash.)

Backdrop DON'TS: a messy bedroom; your gran's chintzy curtains; a kebab shop; a pile of washing up; a man nuzzling into your neck; a bed with leopard print satin sheets.

4. Smile like you mean it: What is it about cameras that turn perfectly gorgeous smiles into Posh-style pouts? It's a common myth among girls that moody equals seductive. Ask any guy and he will tell you there's nothing sexier than a genuine smile.

A smile says that you're fun to be around, happy, positive, down-to-earth, confident, and that you don't take yourself too seriously. A pout suggests you're a miserable, high-maintenance princess.

In particular, steer clear of what I call the 'Facebook cheekbone' shot (hold camera high in the air for the best cheekbone angle/point at yourself and pout).

5. Cut out the competition: Avoid using a group shot for your main profile picture. This is your opportunity to be in the limelight. You don't want someone else stealing your thunder, do you? Just imagine how gutted you'd be if you kept getting enquiries about the fit friend standing next to you!

'I posted a picture of myself with my two best mates as my main shot. I thought it was obvious I was the one in the middle but when the picture was cropped to thumbnail size on the search pages, I was practically cut right out so my gorgeous friend was the focus. I didn't realise this until I started getting emails saying "beautiful red dress". I was wearing black. My friend has now been going out with one of those men for four months – at least I sorted someone's love life out!' Jude, 21, Bristol

6. Avoid 'pap' shots: You don't want your pictures to read like a gossip mag spread of Lily Allen on a 48-hour bender. Falling out of cabs, flashing your knickers, mascara halfway down your face . . . you know the ones. Not a good look, ladies.

You might think you get progressively more attractive after each cocktail but really you don't. You're just seeing yourself in soft focus and sadly cameras don't have an inbuilt beer-goggles function.

7. Bin the bikini shot: I'm sure you do look hot in your skimpy bikini, but the kind of guy who is going to go for a girl based on her body is likely to be interested in one thing only – and it's not your sense of humour. If you're a surfy chick who lives for the beach and you want to give off that vibe, stick to a head and shoulders shot with the ocean as your backdrop.

Needless to say, underwear shots are out of the question. I mean, I'm no prude but that's a different kind of internet dating altogether – and you won't find those sites listed in here I'm afraid.

8. Choose a recent shot: Oh, but you looked so much better on that holiday three years ago when you were really tanned and half a stone skinnier and your hair was really long. That's as may be but if that's not the girl who is going to be turning up on the date, it's false advertising. You will appreciate why this is so wrong when you face your first date with a man who looks nothing like his picture. Oh, and take my word for it, even if you go nil by mouth and strap yourself to a cross trainer for a month before you start dating, you will still not look like you did on that picture. Celebrate who you are *now* – you're gorgeous!

9. Steer clear of the ex: You can spot a cropped-out-ex-boyfriend shot a mile away – you looking blissfully loved up with a mysterious hairy arm around your shoulder. We've all got romantic pasts but the operative word here is past. He doesn't need it rammed down his throat. If the only pictures you can find are of you with your ex then perhaps you need to spend a little bit more time out and about having fun as a singleton before you go looking for your ex's replacement.

10. Beware of the 'bonkers' shot: By this I mean going cross-eyed, gurning, wearing flashing deely boppers or an afro wig and all those other zany madcap antics you and the girls get up to after your tenth glass of rosé. It might convey your GSOH but he's more likely to be thinking WTF? How's he going to know that you look any better when you're not gurning, or that your cross-eyed look isn't a double bluff to hide the fact you are actually cross-eyed?

The more, the merrier

Now you've got your main shot sorted, it's a good idea to think about adding more pictures. This will not only give him a clearer idea of what you look like and therefore more likely to take things to the next stage (you really can't tell from one shot), but it will also give you an opportunity to reveal a little bit more about who you are.

Now you've demonstrated that your eyes, nose and mouth are in the right places and what your hair looks like, you're at liberty to throw the rule-book out of the window and start choosing your favourite shots. Whether it's having a brilliant night out with your friends, trekking up a Himalayan mountain or chilling out at the beach, this is your chance to paint a picture of your life. If it looks like the kind of lifestyle he could get used to, you're onto a winner.

His pictures decoded

The professional moody shot: Everybody looks good in black and white, especially when their face is hidden in shadow. What exactly is this man trying to hide and what's he going to look like in the cold light of day? Plus, if he's spent this long pouting in front of the camera, you'll never get a look-in in the bathroom mirror. This man is in love with someone else. Himself.

The extreme shot: Man standing on top of mountain, man flying through the air on a snowboard, man surfing giant wave. There's something undeniably sexy about men who are into extreme sports, but you're either going to spend your weekends an extreme sports widow or being dragged up mountains/across choppy waters/through the air. If your idea of extreme is running in four-inch heels, this man is not for you.

The lager shot: Beware the red-faced bloke in a football shirt with a can of lager in his hand surrounded by his mates. Particularly if he's wearing some form of novelty hat or a traffic cone on his head, or has vomit on his top. Unless, of course, you're the kind of girl who goes out wearing a feather boa and flashing deely boppers of a Saturday night. Life for you two would be one big party: the biggest, trashiest hen/stag party imaginable.

The corporate office shot: Yawn. OK, so this might be the only shot he had available but something tells me this man is married to his job. He's probably the kind of guy who talks about 'running things up the flagpole' or 'thinking outside the box'. He'd probably rather create his profile as a PowerPoint presentation. Even if he does manage to 'find a window free' to see you, don't expect fireworks. This guy is better in the boardroom than the bedroom, and expect a third party on the date: his BlackBerry.

The wedding shot: There are thousands of internet dating shots out there of men in grey suits with burgundy waistcoats and white carnation buttonholes (a glass of champagne in hand for the really adventurous). This shows absolutely no imagination whatsoever and says zero about the person behind the morning suit. Who knows what they normally wear? This game is about standing out in the crowd. These guys don't deserve a look-in. Having said that this guy could be subconsciously sending out wedding/marriage vibes so if you're looking for a hubby, this one could be a keeper.

The female friend attached: Beware the man who has a cute looking girl draped over him/nuzzling into his neck/getting a piggy back/holding his hand/linking arms with him. Assuming this is not an ex (that would just be downright weird) these two have a very close physical relationship and when you arrive on the scene she is going to be defending her territory so if you have a green-eye monster within, prepare for it to rear its ugly head.

The novelty hat/wig shot: For me this is the pictorial equivalent of using the word 'whacky' or 'zany'. If a man needs to put a giant piece of foam on top of his head in the shape of a pint of Guinness or a bright yellow curly wig in order to let people know he is funny, you can bet your bottom dollar, the one thing he is not is funny. He is likely to be the kind of man who talks over everyone else at group gatherings too.

The sliced-off head shot: This man is probably bald. Of course, there's nothing wrong with being bald. In fact a few of my rather hot male friends have become follically challenged over recent years and it hasn't made a blind bit of difference to their hotness. But baldness is one of those things that can take you by surprise when you're not expecting it. So if you're off for a date with decapitated-head man just be prepared for him to whip off his hat halfway through the evening to reveal a smooth, shiny hair-free head.

The extreme close-up: This man is potentially quite overweight, possibly even morbidly obese, and he doesn't want you to see what he looks like any further out than his eyes, nose and mouth. Not even his chin. Or should I say chins? Is there a full-body shot in any of his other pics? No, I thought not. Check what this man has put under 'build'. Now, I'm not fattist, but I'm just warning you that if you don't like your men cuddly, you might want to give this one a wide berth.

The mug shot: It's a widely acknowledged truth that everybody's passport photo bears an uncanny resemblance to the prison mug shot of a serial killer. Probably even Kylie Minogue's. It would seem nobody is immune to the horrors of the photobooth camera. But the question is, who would put such a shot as their main profile picture on an internet dating site? At best, somebody who looks no better on their holiday snaps than they do in mug-shot mode (not good); at worst, a serial killer.

Let me be a horrible warning #3:
Ask him when his picture was taken

Phil* had texted me on my way to the date to say he'd arrived early and would be waiting on the train platform, so I was surprised to see nobody around when I got there. Well, apart from a rail worker in an orange vest and a homeless man on the floor. As I began to walk towards the exit to find Phil, I felt something tugging on the ankle of my jeans. I looked down. It was the homeless bloke. I went to get my purse out of my bag to give him some change. "Georgia?" he said looking slightly confused. He wasn't homeless. He was Phil.

Unfortunately, Phil had failed to warn me that the shaved head from his photo had grown into a long mop of bright yellow dreadlocks, which was admittedly the perfect complement to the sweeping floor-length army coat and huge military boots he was wearing. The only thing missing was the dog on a string.

When questioned, Phil had to confess that his picture had been taken nine years ago. Judging by the sallow skin, hollow cheeks and dark sunken eyes he'd cultivated in that time, I wasn't surprised to hear he'd had a fairly 'fun-packed' few years. I left Phil in the bar, on the hunt for another party, and haven't seen him since.

CHAPTER 5

Let The Flirting Commence

Now that the very best all-singing, all-dancing, bad-hair-day-free, irresistible, hilarious version of you is out there on show, it's time for the fun and games to begin. Excited?

'I fancy you'

Most sites work in pretty much the same way: Click on the members you like the look of in order to add them to your 'favourites' list, then cross your fingers that the feeling's mutual. This is the virtual equivalent of smiling at a guy across the bar. It means, 'There's something about you that does it for me. I wouldn't mind finding out more . . . if you feel the same.'

Meanwhile, guys will be adding you to their favourites too. Most sites give prominence to new members, so expect a rush at the beginning and don't be put off if things slow down a little once you've dropped off the 'latest profiles' page. As a general rule the most recently active members will be at the front of the queue on searches so the more time you spend logged on, the more visible you'll be to window-shoppers. And we all know what blokes are like when it comes to shopping – they'll go for the first thing they see because they can't be bothered to keep browsing.

Click . . . quick!

So what are you waiting for? Get clicking lady. Hang on, what do you mean you're feeling shy? You look hot! Have you looked at that picture lately? That witty, interesting, charismatic, confident, fun-loving chick you've just been raving about in your profile – that's you. Any man would be chuffed to bits to get attention from you. What? You're waiting for them to make the first move? Hmm, well that's exactly what I was waiting for when I first signed up to this online dating lark, and believe me I'd still be waiting now if I hadn't been told to wake up and smell the competition. So . . .

Wake up and smell the competition

Okay, picture the scene: You've got the party of the year coming up and there are going to be loads of sexy single men there, guaranteed. Not wanting to miss out on a valuable opportunity for some hot loving (with a view to marriage and a fairytale ending), you blow half your salary on a pair of killer heels and a TDF frock. After two hours of battling with fake tan, wax strips and hair straighteners, you emerge like a princess from a pink cloud of lipstick, powder, paint (and perfume), looking (and smelling) a million dollars. But as soon as you get to the party, you spot a cosy little seat in the deepest, darkest corner of the bar that's calling your name ('Come take the weight off those four-inch stilettos!' it cries), so you plant yourself there for the rest of the night, sipping Cosmopolitans and admiring the talent.

Meanwhile Jo Average waltzes in wearing last year's Primark and demonstrating the pitfalls of an overdue hair appointment, only to waltz back out again an hour later with TMOYD (The Man of Your Dreams) in tow. You, on the other hand go home alone, drunk and deflated, listening to the incessant ramblings of the cab driver who wants to know, 'What's a beautiful girl like you doing going home on her own?'. Good question, cabbie. The moral of the story? Don't wear four-inch stilettos when you're out on the pull. Oh, yes, and put yourself out there because you will only ever get back what you put in. If he can't see the radiant smile and killer cheekbones you carefully cultivated for your main profile pic, he ain't gonna be blown away by them, is he? No, he's going to end up settling for second best and dating Make-do Sue – instead of you.

Cast your net wide

It's a really bad idea to be too picky at this stage. If you still have that 378-point boyfriend criteria tick-list in your head, put it aside for now. That's something to reassess come date two. You're not proposing marriage here, you're not even asking the dude to go for a coffee, you're just letting him know his profile shows a bit of promise, and encouraging him to take a look at yours. So give the guy a chance.

If you start being precious about this and treat your favourites page like an elite VIP members' club where only the beautiful people can get in, expect your ego to take a battering. The beautiful people are inevitably the ones who are most inundated and therefore the most likely to blank you. There's nothing more depressing than having a favourites page full of cool, sexy eligible hotties and a fans page full of excess nasal hair, paunches, novelty hats and serial-killer death stares. The profiles in between are where you'll find the hidden gems, but they'll only find you if you make yourself known.

Don't forget, while you may have read my failsafe guide to looking drop-dead gorgeous in your profile picture, he probably hasn't. So don't write someone off based on one grainy postage-stamp sized pic. Once you start dating you'll be faced with the startling reality that very few guys look anything like their pictures anyway, so if in any doubt, click.

Get on the A-list

Another reason to be cavalier with your clicking finger is the more people you add, the more prominence you'll have on the site and therefore the more attention you'll get. On Guardian Soulmates, for instance, the more people you add to your favourites, the more likely you are to accrue fans and the more fans you have the more likely you are to get into the Most Popular section which is flagged up on the site's homepage. When I made it to number 16 for a few days the attention soared. I felt like Sienna Miller – even if I did have to add half the site to my favourites list to get there.

So, swallow your pride ('But I never make the first move') and your prejudice ('But he's wearing a fleece!') and you've got a much better chance of bagging your Mr Darcy.

... but don't get carried away

That said, there's no point adding a guy whose profile is riddled with non-negotiable deal-breakers. If he's a butcher from Glasgow who loves thrash metal, and you're a vegan from Brighton who meditates to whale music, it's never going to work – even if he does have a George Clooney twinkle in his eye. Likewise, don't start adding men just because they've clicked on you and you don't want to hurt their feelings . . .

Let me be a horrible warning #4: Beware of the pity vote

I don't know about you but I've always had a soft spot for the underdog. At school I used to offer my Pickled Onion Monster Munch to Fat Barry, the boy with BO and a wonky eye, because I couldn't bear to see him sitting on his own in the playground. I thought I was making his lonely life that little bit more bearable. It was only when Fat Barry (now incredibly Fit Barry) emailed me on

Facebook recently, I discovered I had in fact been making his life a complete misery. According to Barry my corn snack offerings had been nothing but a cruel tease that he had taken as a symbol of much deeper feelings than pity. So when I withdrew my visits and went off with the captain of the football team, he felt even lonelier than he had done in the first place.

If only Barry had contacted me a little earlier he might have prevented me making the same mistake with online dating. When Roy, a 43-year-old Dungeons and Dragons and Meatloaf fanatic who still lived with his mum, emailed me to say he really liked the look of my picture but didn't expect me to respond because nobody else had, I couldn't bring myself to blank him. But when I finally broke the news after three weeks of avoidance tactics, that a date was never going to happen (tempting as a trip to The London Dungeon sounded), he was not best pleased. I wasn't able to apologise either because not only did he immediately remove me from his favourites list, he put a block on my emails to prevent me from contacting him ever again.

So when it comes to matters of the heart, you have to be cruel to be kind. If you know for sure he has absolutely no chance of going on a date with you, don't add him to your favourites.

'He didn't click me back . . . am I loser?'

No, you are not a loser. But yes, you will probably get rejected and of course nobody likes rejection. But the good news is it happens to everybody (even the girls with the most popular profiles) so it really is nothing personal. There are a million reasons why he might have ignored your request. Maybe he has already met a girl on the site he's having fun with and can't think about anyone else until he's given her a chance. This happens a lot and should be taken as a good thing. If you'd been on a couple of dates with a man and had great banter with him and thought you really liked him, wouldn't it be nice to think he was focused on you and not clicking on every other pretty girl who comes along and adds him as a favourite.

Maybe he has been on 10 dates in the last two weeks and is now taking it easy. When you've been on quite a few dates with unsuitable types it can make you more wary and fussy about who you take that next step with. After all, dating can be a pricey, time-consuming and exhausting business. Also, don't forget, men have tick-lists, too. It could be that he will only go out with Jewish redheads who are under five foot, or maybe you are the spitting image of his evil, cheating ex.

You can analyse it until you're blue in the face but it won't get you anywhere, so my advice is forget about him and move on. Whatever you do, do NOT email him to ask him why.

'Nobody's clicking on me . . . are you sure I'm not a loser?'

It's one thing when the sexiest guys on the site don't respond to your advances but it's another when even the dregs start ignoring you. If you're really having no luck whatsoever, it could be time to reassess your technique:

1. Change your picture

Is that *really* the best picture of you? If in doubt, email a selection to a few of your closest friends and get them to vote for the best one. Even better, include a few male friends if you can. What we think men find attractive and what men really find attractive are often two completely different things. While we're more likely to be concerned with looking slim and seductive, they're more likely to be on the hunt for a girl who looks like she'd be fun to hang out with.

2. Change your clicking tactics

I can't emphasise this enough but you really need to be proactive. The more attention you give to the boys, the more attention you will get back in return. Again, ask one of your friends to look with you. Sometimes they'll see potential you've overlooked.

'When my friend Emma persuaded me to join a dating site my initial reaction was major disappointment at the level of talent. I just wasn't interested in anyone. Yet Emma, who had been on the site for a couple of weeks, had about five dates lined up already. I couldn't understand where the hell she was getting them from so I asked her to point them out. It turned out I had come across all of their profiles already but had dismissed them out of hand – one had a boring job, another was pulling a weird face, another sounded a bit too serious. I felt sorry for poor

Emma. What a week she had in store. I needn't have worried. The one who was pulling a weird face is gorgeous when he's not gurning and has been her boyfriend for almost a year. Luckily for me, she handed over the one with the boring job. He may be a tax accountant but he plays a mean bass guitar.' Jane, 27, Bristol.

3. Are you on the right site?

If things aren't working out, don't give up. Check out some of the other sites out there and browse through their profiles. Each site tends to attract a slightly different set of people so what works for one person doesn't always work for another.

What he really thinks . . .

Do you get offended if you add a girl to your favourites and she doesn't return the compliment?

'What's the point of getting upset? There are loads of gorgeous girls out there. If one doesn't fancy me, that's her loss, not mine.'

'If I really like the look of a girl and she doesn't respond, I send her an email and charm her with one of my witty one-liners. I would say, 50 per cent of the time she gives in. And if she doesn't, nobody could accuse me of not trying.'

'I get more annoyed if she adds me to her favourites but then ignores me when I email her. I'd rather she didn't bother if she's not interested.'

If a girl adds you to her favourites and you don't click back, is that usually because you think she's unattractive?

'Even if a girl is drop-dead gorgeous, I won't bother adding her to my favourites if I don't think we're going to get on. If she's too old or too young or she's religious or she smokes, there's no point. But I'm not going to bother writing to tell her that.'

'If I'm really into someone else on the site I don't bother clicking on other girls until I've given this one a chance. Otherwise things start getting messy!'

What are you thinking when you add a girl to your favourites?

'I'm pretty gung-ho about who I add to my favourites. Sometimes I'll add a girl just because she added me, sometimes it will be based on a funny line she's written in her profile. It doesn't necessarily mean I want to go on a date with her. It takes a couple of emails to work that one out.'

'I don't see the point wasting time writing an email to a girl if she doesn't fancy me so I always test the water first by adding her to my favourites. That's my way of letting her know I'm interested. If she clicks back I'll follow up with an email.'

'I don't bother with adding people to my favourites. I'd rather just send then an email and cut to the chase. Time

is money with this internet dating lark so what's the point in beating around the bush . . . if you'll pardon the pun!'

Decode his profile

Before you add him to your favourites list, check his profile for any hidden telltale signs of trouble. Here are a few 'alarm bells' phrases:

He says: 'I like independent women.'

He means: 'I'll be mostly in the pub with my mates/don't be texting me every five minutes.'

He says: 'I like a drink.'

He means: 'I'm a total booze hound.'

He says: 'Well-built'

He means: 'Lardy'

He says: 'Football is my passion.'

He means: 'Dates must be organised in conjunction with the football fixtures list.'

He says: 'I'm an old fashioned kind of a guy.'

He means: 'A woman's place is in the kitchen.'

He says: 'I'm pretty crazy!'

He means: 'I once stole a traffic cone and wore it on my head.'

He says: 'I'm the life and soul of the party.'

He means: 'You'll usually find me at 4am wearing a feather boa, dancing around the kitchen with a broom singing "New York, New York".'

He says: 'I wud like 2 mt sum1 cool.'

He means: 'I have the mental age of 14.'

He says: 'I like a girl who looks after her appearance and likes to make an effort.'

He means: 'I'm looking for a piece of arm candy who looks like Barbie doll and doesn't have any opinions.'

He says: 'I'm in between jobs.'

He means: 'I'm on benefits.'

He says: 'I'm an entrepreneur.'

He means: 'Del boy'

He says: 'I'm a free spirit.'

He means: 'Don't be surprised if I go AWOL for days on end and don't answer any of your calls, texts or emails.'

He says: 'I'm not looking to rush into anything serious. Let's just see what happens.'

He means: 'Fancy a shag?'

'Help, I've got PMS!'
(Perfect Match Syndrome)

Q: 'Never mind all these people who claim that online dating is seriously uncool. I feel like I'm not cool enough! I have spent so much time reading what men are looking for in their ideal match that I'm starting to feel really inadequate. My friends swear blind I'm lovely and a real catch, but I feel like the most boring girl on the planet. I'm not an extreme sports girl who wants to spend her weekends scaling/cycling over/snowboarding down mountains; I've never worked in an orphanage/been trekking in India; I'm not confident with heavyweight political debates; I can't do cryptic crosswords; I don't read ten books/watch ten films/discover ten new bands a week; I'm more of a domestic disaster than a domestic goddess . . . If I ever went on a date with one of these men I'd feel like one big guilty pleasure. I wouldn't dare tell them I like Coronation Street, have a secret penchant for Hugh Grant films and crisp sandwiches and love a bit of celebrity gossip. I don't stand a chance against the other superwomen on the site. And I know, I've checked out the competition.'
Zoe, 24, Dorset

A: Many dating sites encourage you to describe your 'ideal partner', which seems pretty futile given that we don't live in an 'ideal' world. Perfect matches only exist in fantasyland. Luckily, any bloke worth dating will be well aware of this. On the other hand, any bloke who really believes he is going to find a woman with Cheryl Cole's sweetness, Angelina's Jolie's wickedness,

Carol Vorderman's IQ and Nigella Lawson's muffins should probably sign up for a lifetime's subscription, because she isn't going to show up on an internet dating site any time soon.

It's useful to get an idea of the kind of girl he is looking for, but when scanning profiles don't fall into the trap of focusing on the negatives and honing in on the boxes you don't tick. It's true, there are lots of guys out there who are looking for girls with a sense of adventure and a love of the outdoors but there are just as many looking for girls with a sense of humour. Most importantly, the vast majority don't really know what they are looking for and will only know when they find it.

What he really wants . . .

'Maybe she's blonde . . . hmm, or brunette . . . or she could be a redhead; perhaps she's sporty . . . or more of a chilled-out sort who likes hanging out in cafés . . . in other words, I don't really care as long as she finds me hilarious, smiles a lot and likes exploring new places.' Tim, 29, Cumbria

'How could I possibly know what my ideal match will be like? I haven't met her yet. She could tick every one of the boxes but on the day we just don't click. Likewise she could tick none of them and then blow me away the second she walks into the room.' Adam, 23, West London

'You can't create your ideal match from a list – it's all about the chemistry.' Patrick, 19, Weymouth

'I don't really care which books she reads or what her favourite film is. I do care that she's kind and funny and sexy . . . oh, and red shoes are always a bonus, too (but we can work on that).' Scott, 26, Oxford

Decode his profile: what's your type?

The nice guy
'I'm fun, low maintenance and I won't make you watch football . . . I hold doors open, and generally put toilet seats back down, and the kettle's always just boiled . . . I'm good at fixing things.'

He'll treat you like a princess, but if you like a challenge you'll be tired of this one by date three. If you know you don't like them too sweet, don't mess with this one. He doesn't deserve it.

The cynic
'I'm not lively, optimistic and bubbly; at least, not all the time and never all at the same time. I'm never bubbly. But I can be quite funny, I think; people often laugh at things I say...or perhaps just at me.'

Sarcastic, cynical and a little bit dark, his dry sense of humour can be cruel which is kinda sexy, but his negativity could bring you down after a while. If you're looking for the sunshine of your life, the forecast is not looking good.

The thinker

'I don't like much trash pop culture so unless you have some new angle on it that explains your appreciation, that appreciation could be a stumbling block. I'm also a bit of a crypto-communist, even though I realise revolution is unlikely and I like my bourgeois comforts.'

If you love the finer things in life, listen to Radio 4 and tune in regularly to *Newsnight*, expect evenings based around great food and lively debate. But just remember his opinions are fact. If you know anything about Cheryl Cole's marriage or Posh's waist measurements (i.e. you read *Heat*), expect a very awkward date.

The salt-of-the-earth

'Notwithstanding my devastatingly low standards in films, longing for bouncy castles and penchant for crisp sandwiches (even better with salad cream and beetroot) I guess you could say I'm pretty normal-ish. I'm pretty happy with my life but would like to share it with someone special.'

You can't go far wrong with this man. He'll make you laugh when you've had a crappy day at work, sit through a romcom at the cinema (and secretly like it), text you when he's said he's going to and generally give you very little grief. Of course, that would just be too easy. Where's the drama?

The hopeless romantic

'I'm looking for a soulmate; a special someone who can warm my heart with one smile; a girl with a twinkle in her eye to share the good times; someone to walk into the sunrise of my life with; someone who wears their heart on their sleeve and isn't afraid to love . . . '

Well, you're not going to be in any doubt about whether he's into you or not, that's for sure. If it's romance you're looking for, this is your man. Prepare for many hours spent gazing into one another's eyes. Be warned though, romantic souls who throw themselves into relationships and fall hard and fast often are often more in love with the idea of the relationship than the relationship itself, and once reality sets in the bubble bursts.

CHAPTER 6

How To Give Good Email

Most dating sites have an internal email system. This is a great opportunity to learn a little bit more about him, and get a better idea of how compatible you are, before committing to a face-to-face encounter. But be warned, clicking with someone in the virtual world is certainly no guarantee you'll click on the date.

Two things to bear in mind before you hit send . . .

1. Don't fake it

With the internet at your fingertips, it can be quite tempting to fake a funnier, smarter, more interesting version of the real you, with the help of your very own online spin-doctors (Google, Wikipedia, MySpace, YouTube . . .). For instance, when he's rambling on about some far-flung expedition he went on during his gap year and you haven't the foggiest whether it's in

Asia, Africa or America, you can simply type it into Google maps and bingo. Look it up on Wikipedia and you can even impress him with a surprising statistic or quirky fact. Never heard of that obscure band he's talking about? Hello MySpace. Don't know any of the films by that director? imdb.com will tell you . . .

This is all very well, but unless you arrange to meet in a wi-fi zone and have your iPhone tucked up your sleeve for emergency web searches in the Ladies, you will have to leave your IQ-boosting online assistants at home and rely on your own natural charm and wit when it comes to the date. So beware of creating an irresistible alter ego – he might be disappointed when she's nowhere to be seen on the right.

2. Don't fall in love . . . yet!

Without any of those first-date anxieties and inhibitions to hold you back ('is my hair a mess?'/'what if I run out of things to say?'/'I'm having a sense of humour failure'), it's much easier to be witty, charming and confident on email. So it's not surprising that virtual relationships can be highly addictive. But remember, you are only getting an edited version of the real person you're chatting to. What's more, no matter how well you get on over email, you can never predict if the chemistry will be there when you meet. If you've reached the point where your tummy flips over every time his name appears in your inbox, it's time to take things offline and find out if he has the same effect in person.

Let me be a horrible warning #5: Don't get carried away

I was sitting in a café with my laptop when Matt* popped up in my inbox. His opening line was so funny I snorted tea up my nose while trying to contain my laughter. This was quite possibly the funniest email I'd ever read. His picture was cute, too. I was hooked. I sent him what I hoped was a witty reply and there marked the start of a beautiful e-relationship. From that moment we were 'virtually' inseparable – before the start of work, in our lunch breaks, every evening until the early hours...The more we bantered, the more flirtatious things got and the more addictive it became. There was only one problem: I was living in Barcelona and he was living in London. I had only really logged on to the site for research purposes for this book, but because I knew I'd be returning to London a month later I thought a bit of banter wouldn't do any harm. By the time we finally got to meet, things had become so intense I had practically worked out the wedding seating plan. But that was okay, he ticked all the boxes. What could possibly go wrong?

It was hard to say what did go wrong really, except that as soon as we sat down, we both froze. Matt was a bit more 'well built' than he looked in his picture and the confident, cheeky chappy I'd just spent the past month falling for was nowhere to be seen. I had met more cheerful looking passport controllers. Judging by the way he was ripping his beer mat to shreds, furtively

> looking around the room and shifting in his seat, I don't think he was struggling to suppress lustful thoughts about me either. It was a relief to say goodbye to the real Matt at the end of the night, but it took me a good few weeks to get over the loss of the virtual man of my dreams.

Safety and security

The internal email systems on dating sites are there for a reason – privacy and security – so use them. Don't give out your personal email address until you're sure about him. Be cautious about giving away your surname too as this will allow him to do internet searches on you (not that we would ever do that, of course – Google a new man, what do you mean?). Likewise, hold off on Facebook 'friending' until you've got to know him a bit better. Besides, do you really want him to see those trashy hen night pictures before you meet him?

His email style decoded: 1

The me me me-mail
'Hi, I just got back from another tough day at the office. It's pretty intense being the head of an international export company but I thrive on the challenge and every time I get into my Porsche and drive back to my riverside penthouse flat it all seems

worth it; but that's not before I've done three hours' triathlon training on the way home. The training certainly pays off though, I'm not sure I'm going to be able to fit my next triathlon champion's trophy in the display cabinet. My friends marvel how I manage to fit so much into my life and still manage to be the life and soul of the party and do all that charity work. I like to give 110 per cent with everything I do...'

This man has absolutely no interest in you or any other woman for that matter. He is in the midst of a lifelong love affair with himself. But he feels it's selfish to keep him all for himself, and being the charitable type has decided it's time to share some of his good fortune with you. He would like to put himself centre stage in your display cabinet so you too can admire him and benefit from being close to him. You lucky thing, you.

If the email reads like a sound bite from *The Apprentice,* ignore 110 per cent of its content and delete it. This man will do nothing for your confidence. A date with him will feel like a job interview, with you as the prospective employer as you listen to him bang on about how great he is. The only enjoyment you will get from it will be telling him at the end that he hasn't got the job.

Send, send, send . . .

The same rule applies to emailing as adding people to your favourites – the more messages you send, the more you'll receive. After all, it seems a little pointless to play hard to get when you're on an internet dating site. So, ditch any archaic ideas that men should make the first move because it will get you nowhere in this situation. There are plenty of women on the site who will be only too happy to muscle in and nab your man while you're waiting for him to contact you.

. . . yes, even if he didn't add you as a favourite

Just because he hasn't clicked on you doesn't mean he isn't interested. He might not have spotted you yet. In fact, his mouse might just be hovering over your profile when, ping! a box comes up saying 'Foxxy_Lady has sent you a message'. By the time he's finished concocting a witty reply to Foxxy's flirtatious little message, you've been lost in the ether, never to be seen again.

Sending an email is a great way to get his undivided attention. When he's scanning profile after profile, it's easy to get overlooked. But if you've gone to the trouble of sending him a personal email he'll be flattered by the attention and will most likely at least check out your profile and your extra pictures.

Make it personal . . .

While it's a good idea to send out lots of emails, never go for quantity over quality. Five carefully thought-out personal emails tailored to the person you're writing to are worth 500 generic emails that you've copied and pasted to the entire site. Likewise five words that refer directly to something he has written in his profile shows more thought than 500 words of waffle that could apply to anyone. Even if you have remembered to change the name each time (you'd be surprised how many people forget), blanket emails can be spotted a mile away and usually get relegated to the trash.

His email style decoded: 2

The one with extra cheese

'Hi beautiful, I saw your stunning picture and just had to email you immediately. Your lips so soft and full like strawberries, your eyes like the bluest . . . blueberries. What lucky man will get to kiss those strawberry lips? And not just a pretty face. Your profile made me feel warm inside. The words flowed like a stream of golden champagne cascading down one of those waterfall towers made out of champagne glasses that you sometimes get at weddings and big parties in marquees. I would like to wine you, dine you and have you experience one of my legendary back rubs . . .'

This man is very likely to have a dark tan, some large items of gold jewellery suspended from his person and half a tub of grease in his hair. For a first date expect to be taken to a dark cavernous bar where he will be waiting at a table in the deepest, darkest corner. Personal space is not a phrase this man is familiar with. An evening with him would be like going on a date with an over-excited octopus. You would be lucky to escape alive.

> Sleazy men like this can be quite persistent, so ignoring him might not be enough of a hint. If possible email him back with a short but firm message that makes it clear he will never under any circumstances be standing within five miles of 'your perfectly round breasts'. Don't actually say that though. 'I met someone on here yesterday, we fell in love last night and are planning to get married in Vegas next Wednesday' should suffice. If not, use the 'block this user' tool to prevent further contact.

Beware embarrassing typos

If you've gone to the trouble of writing a decent word perfect profile, don't let yourself down by dropping the standard for your emails. Sending out a message that's littered with typos and spelling mistakes suggests you can't be bothered to make the effort. If in doubt, refer to the spelling and grammar section on page 49.

Also be aware that something as simple as a misspelt word could lead to all kinds of misunderstandings. I was slightly alarmed, for instance, to read budding chef Sam's opening gambit to me: 'I've been told I'm a great cock but I guess you'll have to taste for yourself.'

Don't try too hard

While it's good to put some thought into your emails and add the personal touch, don't spend too long agonising over it. Keep things relaxed and spontaneous and try to write just as you would talk in conversation with your friends. This will give him a good indication of how you'd be on a date. If your message reads as though you've just swallowed a dictionary, it will give the impression you're desperate to impress him. Which maybe you are, but what could be more impressive than an easy-breezy chilled-out chick?

Avoid name-dropping, too. He doesn't need to know a list of every book you've read, film you've watched or exhibition you've seen this month or how many miles you ran before work this morning.

Keep it short but sweet

Even if he has added you as a favourite, you can't be sure how interested he is at this stage. If you spend an hour composing a 300-word email you're only going to feel even more disappointed if you don't get a reply. Think of this as chatting up a guy in the bar. If you stand 3mm away from his face telling him all about your day and firing questions at him, he's going to back away and run for the loo at the first given opportunity. Whereas if you stand next to him at the bar and make a little quip about the hat he's wearing or something funny about the barman, it will be just enough to tell him you're interested without seeming too keen. Throw the ball back into his court.

Grab his attention

Blokes love to spend hours scouring the net for bizarre video footage, weird websites, useless pieces of infor-mation and random facts and statistics. This is probably so they can show off to each other down the pub. So, if you can surprise him with something he didn't already know – especially if it's about a subject he's interested in, he'll be well impressed. Links to cool or funny websites and YouTube videos are guaranteed to get his attention. Plus, it will give you a conversation starting point.

His email style decoded: 3

The copy-and-paste job

'Hi, I liked the look of your profile and thought I'd say hi. My name's Ben. I'm a friendly laid-back guy. I like exploring the city and everything it has to offer but sometimes I like to escape to the countryside, too. I like to party sometimes but equally I'm quite happy in front of a DVD with a bottle of wine. If you like the sound of my profile, please get in touch. If not, happy hunting.'

You didn't like the look of my profile, you haven't even read it. Well, maybe you had a quick look at the pictures to double check I didn't have a beard or a third eye, and then you just sent me the same email you sent the rest of the clean-shaven two-eyed girls on the site. If I were to test you with a little quiz based on my profile you would probably score a big fat zero . . . unless one of the questions was, 'Do I have a beard or a third eye?'

It's quite a polite email and it even wishes you luck if you're not interested, so being a complete sucker I would probably end up sending a polite reply, but to be honest he doesn't really deserve one and let's face it he wouldn't even notice. You're just one of the masses to him.

Keep the conversation flowing

To give him a reason to write back always include at least one question in your emails. If you're stuck for something to ask, refer back to his last email or his profile and go for his favourite topic – himself!

There seems to be a real trend at the moment for online daters to ask those obscure personality-revealing questions, like, 'if you were a tree, what kind of tree would you be and why?' or 'if you could be any character from history who would it be and why?' Personally, I hate those questions. It makes me feel as though I'm in a job interview. My mind always goes blank under the pressure of trying to come up with something deep and philosophical or brilliantly witty. I've even ignored emails from perfectly attractive men simply because I didn't have the time or inclination to think of witty answers to their questions.

You don't need to be too clever about it. As long as you avoid the following subjects, you can't go far wrong: Marriage, children, commitment, exes, money, sex.

Flirty talk v dirty talk

A little bit of harmless flirting is all part of the fun. But be wary of taking things too far. I'm all for a bit of virtual innuendo, but a text-sex situation with someone you already know is slightly different to having virtual sex with a complete stranger on the internet. Apart from the obvious dangers, just think how you're going to feel if you don't fancy him on the date. Also, in your imagination, you may well have the moves of a pole dancer and him the stamina of Superman, but that's a lot of performance pressure when you do finally hit the sack.

'Neil* and I got completely carried away when we started emailing each other late one Saturday night. We'd both just got back from nights out with our mates so we were feeling a bit frisky. The chat started out quite innocently until I told him someone in the bar had spilt wine down my top. It all degenerated from there really. I won't go into details but let's just say I spent a large part of that weekend in bed with my laptop. When we did finally meet up for drinks later the following week we were so excited about living out our fantasies I'm afraid to say we were back at his place two drinks later. But as soon as we hit the bedroom the reality was very different. Neil was clearly embarrassed about his generous descriptions of his vital statistic, and the sight of me looking nervous in a pair of slouchy vintage boots didn't quite match his vision of a dominatrix in thigh-highs. The sex was pedestrian, and so our first date marked the end of our relationship.' Claire, 21, Sheffield

WARNING: Not suitable for use with alcohol

It's 12.30am and you just got back from the pub . . . alone. What's more, your flatmate has come back with an Adonis. But hey, the night's not over yet. Your pulling potential still has legs so let's go and see who's online. This is when you need to *step away from the machine*! Drinking while online is a bit like drinking while on antibiotics – at the time, you think it won't do any harm, but you're sorry when you wake up the next day with an inflamed septic throat . . . or in this case an ignored email.

His email style decoded: 4

Single white email

'Hi, it's me again. Sorry to stalk you but I didn't hear back from the last two emails and just wanted to check you got them. Could you just email me to let me know you've got this one? My computer has been playing up lately and I get the feeling not all my emails are getting through. I'd hate to think I'd missed out on a chance with you because you never got my message. Anyway, as I said in my other messages I just think you sound lovely and think we'd be a great match. We have so much in common. I like music, too, and films and the countryside. I'd love to take you away for the weekend somewhere beautiful where we could curl up in front of a roaring open fire . . . '

Go and have a look outside your window. Can you see any movement behind that car opposite? Can you see someone running away very fast down the street? I'm sure this man has the best of intentions and would genuinely love to make you happy for the rest of your life but his desperation is pretty creepy. You can't help thinking he's already worked out baby names and retirement plans with you. Okay, so you've done the same thing yourself with that guy you put into your

---

favourites list last week but at least you haven't emailed him three times. You haven't, right?

The trouble is we're all hypocrites when it comes to matters of the heart. We're all capable of having those stalkerish thoughts, but acting on them is a different matter. You have to be firm with this one. Tell him you are out of the country indefinitely then change the locks.

Roll with the punches

Don't be too surprised if a guy you thought you were getting on with like a house on fire suddenly stops emailing you. Remember, he will be emailing, and most likely dating, other girls on the site apart from you so situations can change at any moment. This is another good reason to take things offline as soon as you can before some forward little madam gets in there first.

If he hasn't replied to your email, leave it. Chasing him with a follow-up message is unlikely to give you the result you want. 'But, but, I'm not sure it definitely sent, my computer's been playing up recently . . . ' Face facts: Your email does work. He did receive it. It wasn't a communication breakdown at his end. He knows you're interested loud and clear. If he's interested in you he'll be in touch. If he isn't, it's not happening. That's not to say he thinks you're fat/doesn't like that crooked front tooth, hated your profile. It just means right now you're not the girl on his mind.

The worst 10 opening lines from blokes ('Delete! Delete! Delete!')

1. *'Fancy coming for a spin in my Ferrari sometime? You can see a picture of it on my profile'*

Um, no sorry, I'm watching my carbon emissions . . . by the way, is it true what they say about men with flashy sports cars having small penises?

2. *'Hi Jane'*

Who the hell is Jane?

3. *'Hi there, so maybe you'd like to tell me some stuff about you.'*

Um, I already have. In my profile. You're the one contacting me, you tell me!

4. *'Hey Georgia, let me take you on a date, I will slay dragons for you . . . and I know how to run a girl a bath'*

The only running going on on that date would be me running the hell away.

5. *'Hi, here's my phone number, what's yours?'*

Sorry, do I know you? Clearly a man who knows nothing about foreplay.

6. *'Wow, you look just like my ex-girlfriend!'*

I suggest if you really want to get over her you find someone who doesn't.

7. *The shot of me in the wetsuit with the big trophy was taken after a surfing championship. Perhaps I could tell you more about it over a dinner?'*

I'll book a table for three, shall I? You, me and your ego.

8. *'I'm new to this online dating thing so not really sure what I'm supposed to write here . . . '*

Yeah, yeah, skip to the end.

9. *'Hi, I'd like to tell you a little bit about myself. As it says in my profile I run a property company with approx 10 staff. I've worked hard to achieve this . . . '*

Zzzzzzzzz . . .

10. *'Snow or beach?'*

Oh god, not another one of those questions . . .

His email style decoded: 5

Words fail me
'Hi, how are you?'

I wonder how long it took him to come up with that one. This raconteur is sure to have you captivated on the date with his hilarious tales . . . ooh, for at least as long as it takes for you to take your coat off. My suggestion is, don't take it off, you'll be needing it again very soon. I just hope his best mate has got a back-up plan for the Best Man's speech.

There is no excuse for an email this unimaginative. You can't blame being shy – he doesn't even have to deliver the line in person. This is just plain lazy. If it's any indication of his performance in the bedroom, forget it.

Guys on email behaviour

'I get really turned off by too many exclamation marks and smiley faces and LOLs. It's like talking to a child.' Jim, 21, Cardif

'I hate it when a girl doesn't reply after you've been bothered to send a personal and friendly email. A thanks but no thanks is better than nothing.' Paul, 28, Bolton

'I get a bit freaked out when girls get moody if you don't reply within 24 hours. If they're like that already, what are they going to be like if you start seeing them?' Simon, 24, Brighton

'I once received an email from a girl that was the length of a short novel. Clearly, I wouldn't get a word in edgeways on the date.' Nick, 26, West London

CHAPTER 7

It's A Date!

So, you've cracked the online part, now it's time for the tricky bit – dating. For the majority of us, the idea of spending an entire evening making small talk with a complete stranger is about as appealing as going to the dentist for a filling. Except at least with a filling you have the perfect excuse for an awkward silence.

But really, what's the big deal? Most of us chat to people we hardly know on a daily basis without even thinking about it, whether it's the cute guy in Starbucks serving your morning coffee, a friend of a friend you've just been introduced to at a party or the bloke from accounts you keep bumping into in the lift. The only difference is that with spontaneous chats you don't have time to work yourself up into a panic and put a spanner in the works with your own negative thoughts.

First dates are a walk in the park (or a drink in the bar) with a little bit of advanced preparation and the understanding that it's only a chat – you never have to see the guy again.

Are you ready to go offline?

This really depends on the individual. Some guys simply aren't into email banter, or prefer to cut to the chase to find out whether you have that all-important chemistry before getting carried away, while others like to take their time and get to know you before committing to a date (although if he still hasn't asked you out after a month of emailing it's probably time to start asking questions). Only you will know when the time is right to take things to the next stage, so the best thing is to go with your gut instinct. That said, you should certainly suss him out over at least a few emails first, and never feel pressured into meeting someone before you're ready.

Location, location, location

When it comes to the perfect date scenario it's very much a case of horses for courses. If you're both tee-total extreme sports freaks, for instance, a night in a bar isn't going to make for a very relaxing evening. The key is to find an environment that will put you both at your ease.

The coffee/lunch date

Pros: This is a great first-date option because if there's no spark, you've got the perfect excuse to vanish after an hour, if there *is* a spark, you'll both leave wanting more, and if the chemistry's so overwhelming you can't tear yourselves away, you can move on somewhere else and see where the rest of the day takes you. It's a win,

win situation. Plus, with a coffee date there is no fear of any embarrassing alcohol-fuelled misdemeanours.

Cons: It can take a while for the conversation to get into full flow on a first date so if you're on a tight turnaround on your lunch break, you might find you have to cut it short just as things are getting interesting. Also, while getting blotto on the first date is an absolute no-no, a glass of wine can certainly help to take the edge off pre-date nerves. Alcohol-free dates can be quite intimidating if you're the shy or nervous type. Remember caffeine exacerbates anxiety too, so if you're already feeling jittery you could do worse than to order a soothing camomile tea.

The pub date
Pros: If you want an easy, relaxed first date with no stress or pressure, you can't go far wrong with a decent boozer. Try to find somewhere that's lively enough to offer a distraction from any awkward silences, but quiet enough for you to get a seat and be able to communicate without the need for sign language. I love those old-fashioned cosy, cavernous places because they have a romantic vibe, but not in such an obvious way that would make things uncomfortable if you're not feeling the love.

Cons: Choose the wrong pub at the wrong time and you could end up standing squashed in the corner of a packed, noisy, sweaty bar, shouting small-talk and 'Sorry?' 'What?' for the entire night. For this reason, research is key. If in doubt, go for somewhere one of you is familiar with. But not so familiar you're likely to be joined by all his footy mates or your ex. Also, check whether they have any theme nights on. A pub quiz or an Elvis karaoke night could ruin a potentially romantic evening . . . or save a disastrous one.

The gig

Pros: Perfect if you're both into gigs and like the same music. Unlike at the cinema or theatre, you can still chat and wander around or go to the bar. But because you have the band to focus on you don't need to do too much yelling over the noise. If you don't really fancy each other the pressure is off as you're not staring across a table face to face and you can easily get through half an hour in the pub later by talking about the band. If you do fancy each other, you get to have a bit of a dance together and share a memorable experience.

Cons: Gigs can be pretty overwhelming places and not everybody likes to enjoy them in the same way. Personally I like to stand halfway back and just to the side so I'm in with the action and get a view of the stage without being pushed and shoved around too much. The last time I went on a gig-date, he insisted on dragging me through the mosh-pit to the front. I emerged an hour later with only one shoe and a broken toe.

The dinner

Pros: You're guaranteed a seat (you have booked a table, right?), you've got an instant conversation starter (the food), you can enjoy a couple of glasses of wine (without fear of getting inebriated from drinking on an empty stomach) and it's a civilised environment for a decent chat. As with the pub date, it's all down to the venue research. Personally, I find dinner a little bit too intense for a first date. I like the idea of being able to escape at a moment's notice without fear of letting good food go to waste. If you are dining out on date one, go for somewhere informal, inexpensive and relatively lively.

Cons: The menu is a potential minefield: You can't have anything too messy that could lead to food on your face or your new top, so shellfish and spaghetti are off-limits for starters. Spicy foods are always a risk – will it blow your mouth off, or worse, have you blowing off, later? Then, of course, there's the garlic issue if a goodnight kiss is on the cards. Even if you do manage to get through the meal with no major issues, you still have the bill to contend with. Unless he has specifically offered to foot the bill beforehand, never agree to go somewhere you can't afford to pay half. Washing dishes in the kitchen is no way to end a date.

The 'activity' date

Pros: Sports and activities are great ice-breakers. Whether it's bowling, ice-skating, mountain biking or go-karting, you're pretty much guaranteed to have a banter-filled date. A little bit of friendly competition is always good fodder for flirting – and if you're truly useless at the chosen activity it will at least show you're game for a laugh and don't take yourself too seriously.

Cons: If you're the kind of girl whose idea of extreme sport is running for a cab in four-inch heels or who feels queasy at the sight of a broken nail, you're probably better off sticking to something more sedate. Activity dates are not the most glamorous. Many blokes would probably agree that a woman is at her sexiest when she ditches her make-up and her inhibitions. But hey, you could always save that for another time . . . like date 23. Not many men would find the sight of a woman having a tantrum about a broken nail very sexy.

Pre-date DOs and DON'Ts

DO: Leave enough time to get ready
If you're meeting straight from work, give yourself a bit of chill-out time to get ready and wind down before you dash out. If your boss has a tendency to dump a load of work on you five minutes before you're due to leave, factor that in – or make it clear earlier in the day you'll need to leave on time.

DON'T: Allow time for the nerves to set in
While you don't want to be turning up looking hot and flustered, nor do you want to be sitting around twiddling your thumbs and working yourself up into a pre-date panic.

DO: Create a pre-date playlist
Listening to your favourite feel-good tracks is guaranteed to boost your happiness levels and liven you up

---

after a draining day at work. You can't go wrong with a little dance around your room while you're getting ready. If not, make sure your iPod's fully charged for an instant fix of good vibes before you arrive.

DON'T: Get drunk the night before
Ever feel as though you're at your most relaxed and wittiest the morning after a massive night out? That's because you're still drunk. Once the alcohol has left your bloodstream you'll be a bleary-eyed wreck.

DO: Meet up with a friend beforehand
Having a bit of a giggle will put you in a good mood. Choose the mate who always makes you feel good about yourself. She can tell you how fabulous you look and remind you that if it doesn't work out it's no big deal because you've got brilliant friends to hang out with, anyway.

DON'T: Get drunk beforehand
That first glass of wine has been scientifically proven to send your brain's serotonin soaring, but while you might arrive on the date feeling more confident and less nervous you will also be one step closer to getting drunk. If you do want a drink to calm your nerves, make it a small wine or a single spirit. No Sambuca chasers.

Chill-out, it's no big deal

If you turn up to every date with the expectation that this is going to be the start of a long and meaningful relationship, you're missing half the fun and will probably find yourself on quite a few depressing bus journeys home. Of course, it's only natural that in the back of your mind you're hoping to meet someone, that's why you've joined the site but what's wrong with getting your money's worth and enjoying the dating part? You have a fantastic opportunity here to do some serious boy shopping. The shelves are packed, so have a good look at what's on offer and try a few things on for size before rushing into your big purchase.

If you approach each date as a bit of a laugh with a new mate and forget about what might or might not happen after the date you'll have a whole lot more fun. So what if he doesn't make it to round two? It doesn't mean you've wasted an evening, it just means you've become that little bit more accomplished at the art of dating. Getting out of your comfort zone and learning to enjoy the company of new people is a great way to build confidence, and not only for your love life. As a dating columnist, I've been on more blind dates than I care to remember, many of which were more painful than a Brazilian wax, but as a result, I'm rarely stuck for words when it comes to making small-talk at parties and can flirt my way out of the most tricky situations. ('Sorry Mr Cabbie, I think the cash machine short-changed me.')

Let me be a horrible warning #6:
Don't expect to meet The One on date one

I threw myself into online dating with the greatest of expectations. But after a rollercoaster week of excitement and disappointment, I soon learned to take each date as it comes.

MONDAY: David* sounded amazing – and he was taking me to see my favourite band. Result. I had a good feeling about this one. I clocked him immediately, sitting at the bar with a pint. I walked over and leaned in for a peck on the cheek but as I did he slipped off the bar stool and vanished from sight. His eyes were now level with my cleavage. Yes, he was shorter standing up than he was sitting down. I felt a wretched mixture of guilt (how could I be so shallow?) and disappointment (how could he be so small?). He was lovely though, and the Kings of Leon gig was amazing, but I found myself wondering if I should offer to let him sit on my shoulders. It just didn't feel right.

TUESDAY: After an hour of Rich* droning on about his ex-girlfriend, he lunged towards me for a kiss. I pulled away, knocking his drink over his crotch. 'I'm so sorry', he sobbed, his eyes welling with tears, his groin welling with Guinness. 'You just really look like my ex. That's why I contacted you – I thought it was fate.' I left Rich with a hug and a packet of Kleenex.

WEDNESDAY: When John* said he'd buy me a drink after work, I assumed he meant a glass of wine, not a bottle. I was even more surprised when I returned from the loo less than half an hour later to find he'd bought a second bottle. 'I'm having one more small glass and that's it', I said, beginning to feel slightly warm and woozy. When I came back from the Ladies a second time to see two Sambucas lined up on the table, I said, 'Rohypnol would have been cheaper' and stumbled out.

THURSDAY: I was tired, hungover and over it, but when Mark* walked into the bowling alley, my jaw dropped. He was hot, funny, charming – and my God, didn't his bum look cute when he was bowling? I had finally met my match and I was pretty sure I was in with a chance.

FRIDAY: I stared at my phone all day waiting for a text from Mark. I received one at 11.30pm. It read: 'Sorry, probably should have told you, but I am kind of seeing someone. You're cute, though, I could come to your flat.'

Stick it in your bag . . .

Mints
Bye, bye garlic . . . hello goodnight kiss.

Concealer
'Where the hell did that come from?' Spots have a habit of gatecrashing dates.

Mobile
With your best mate and a trusted cab firm on speed dial . . . just in case.

Fully loaded wallet
'Ooh, I forgot my wallet!' is not going to wash. Allowing him to pay is fine. Expecting him to pay is not.

Deodorant/perfume
You want to be hot under the collar, not under the armpits.

Condoms . . .
. . . If there is even the slightest chance you're going to have sex.

Plasters
New shoes? Hobbling like an injured footballer is *so* not a good look.

Leave it out of your bag . . .

Your heavy-duty 5kg make-up bag
You want him to think you look like that naturally.

Self-help books
Having *How To Make Him Fall In Love With You* poking out of your bag will teach you exactly How To Make Him *Not* Fall In Love With You.

Pictures of your kitten/hamster/niece
Fluffy will not have the same heart-melting effect on him as he does on you.

Super-sized box of Tampons
We all use them, but nobody wants to think about them while they're eating.

Chemistry lessons

'I couldn't possibly describe my ideal match. I guess I'll just know when we meet. It's all down to chemistry.'
Justin, 26, Fife

You will see plenty of lines like this as you're browsing the boys' profiles. It would appear while us ladies are fussy when it comes to details such as height and career, the men are more interested in animal instinct and the holy grail of romance – chemistry. But what is chemistry? Does it have to hit you on date one like a thunderbolt as soon as your eyes meet or is it something that can develop further down the line? And is it really a vital ingredient for every relationship?

Lesson 1: Chemistry alone isn't enough
When we are attracted to someone, our bodies are invaded by all manner of crazy chemical reactions. For romantics like me it's easy to confuse those early feelings of lust with something deeper. But fancying the pants off each other is not enough to sustain a long-term relationship if you can't even decide where to go for a coffee without bickering.

Lesson 2: Chemistry isn't always mutual
If chemistry were a reciprocal thing, there would be no need for dating sites. But sadly life is not that simple. The sight of your smile might be sending tingles down his spine while the sight of his is sending shudders down yours. Likewise, while you're wondering whether or not you'll get a cheeky snog later, he might be wondering

whether or not he's going to make it home in time for *Match of the Day*. Bear this in mind before you make any moves.

Lesson 3: Chemistry can develop later

First-date nerves can be a real passion-killer so, don't write anyone off too quickly. If in doubt, give him a second chance. It's almost impossible not to arrive on a date with pre-conceived ideas about the 'type' you're likely to fall for. If he is nothing like the men you've gone for before it can take a while to come around to the idea of being attracted to something different.

'When I first met Marcus I didn't fancy him at all. In fact I thought he seemed a bit irritating. He was wearing a stupid hat with earflaps and kept making "dad" jokes, while I like my men with a dry wit. It was only through sheer persistence he persuaded me to give him another go. I don't know what happened during that week but as soon as I arrived on the second date, I was smitten. He seemed much more laid back without the first-date nerves and his crappy jokes had been replaced by razor-sharp one-liners. All I could think throughout the evening was how much I wanted him to kiss me. So I was gutted when we said goodbye and he didn't. In fact, I had to wait until the end of the fourth date before he finally made his move. Apparently, my hard-to-get behaviour at the beginning had made him wary of making a fool of himself. He needn't have worried. The nerd in the stupid hat now shares a flat with me and the hat lives in my wardrobe. Shoved right at the back, thankfully.' Lainey, 25, Nottingham

Lesson 4: Chemistry doesn't live at the bottom of a wine glass

'Chemistry' often has a funny habit of emerging after the third or fourth glass of wine. This is possibly because you've both relaxed, and are now at ease with one another. But there is also the possibility you're just wearing your rosé-tinted spectacles. Come to mention it, the spotty, teenage glass-collector is beginning to look kind of cute, right? My advice on this one is, if you didn't fancy him when you were sober, don't make any decisions about him while you're drunk. Invite him out for a coffee in a few days' time and see if you still feel the same.

First-date etiquette

Chivalry: Dead, dead sweet or dead sexist?

Okay, so you're an independent woman of the noughties. You believe in equal pay, equal rights and equal access to the TV remote control, right? Go sister. But let me guess, when you're sussing out a man on the first date he gets extra brownie points for opening the door for you and you workshop it with your best mate when he doesn't offer to pay? I thought as much. Welcome to the world of dating double standards!

On the subject of chivalry, I think Venus gives poor Mars a bit of a rough deal. The poor guy can't do right for doing wrong. So next time you're putting his first-date manners before the jury (your mates), spare a thought to what might be going through his head. If the scene below sounds familiar, it could be time you started cutting your date a bit of slack. You can always tighten the leash later when he's hook, line and sinker!

Mars: 'Shall I get there early? Girls don't like waiting in pubs on their own, do they? I'll get there 15 minutes early.'

Venus: 'Hmm, second thoughts this top's too booby, back to the red top. I'll miss the train but he won't mind it's a girl's prerogative to be late, right? Anyway, it's only 15 minutes late.'

Mars: 'Will she expect me to pay? The place she's picked is pretty pricey. It's going to wipe me out. She seems pretty independent. I think they like to go Dutch don't they? I don't want her to think I'm sexist.'

Venus: 'He could have at least offered to pay. Obviously I would have insisted on going Dutch but that's not the point. So it's confirmed: chivalry is dead.'

Mars: 'Oh God, isn't it supposed to be the manly thing to take control and order the wine. But I don't know anything about wine. Ooh, I think she's going to the bathroom. I'll get the waiter to help me choose something to impress her.'

Venus: 'I can't believe he's ordered the wine without asking me. I don't even like Chardonnay. Typical man. He's obviously a controlling retro-sexual. He'll be telling me my dress is too short next.'

Mars: 'She seems to be getting a bit flirty. I think she likes me. It would be a shame to cut the night short. I'll ask her if she wants to go on for a night-cap.'

Venus: 'He's trying to get me drunk. It's so obvious. He only wants one thing. Well, he can think again.'

Mars: 'We'll never get a cab around here. I'll lend her my coat and walk her home. She'll like that.'

Venus: 'The coat trick. That old chestnut. You're not getting your way with me tonight pal. I really thought he liked me but no he's just like the rest. I've had enough.'

Mars: 'I really like this girl. I'm going to ignore those stirrings down there. It's a peck on the cheek then I'm off. Then I'll ask her out again in three days. Do it properly. I don't want to lose this one.'

Venus: 'I can't believe he turned down my offer of a coffee. The humiliation. He doesn't fancy me. I hate men. They're so selfish. What a prick!'

How to end the date . . .

. . . when you can't wait to get the hell away

I once went on a date with a guy who left without even finishing his first beer. Maybe he met the woman of his dreams the night before or was suddenly in the grip of an embarrassing case of the trots. I guess I will never know. But what I do know is that I was mortified. It left me feeling like crap and for a good couple of weeks I stopped dating.

No matter how horrendous the date, there is no excuse for being rude. Most of us have faced an ignored call or a lame-excuse text at one time or another, but being rebuffed while you're still on the date is a different matter altogether. The best way to avoid hurting anybody's feelings is to make it clear at the beginning of the date that you've got something else planned later and will need to leave after an hour. You can always change your mind later if things are going well.

Forget arranging the emergency text from your best friend that suddenly and mysteriously calls you away. He will never buy it and will feel not only rejected but ridiculed, too.

... when you don't want the date to end

Congratulations! You've had a blinder of a blind date and everything's gone swimmingly. So swimmingly, in fact, you don't want it to finish. You know the chemistry is mutual because he's started saying things like, 'one more drink and then we'll go' and 'just another cheeky one?' and 'one more for the road?' In fact, you're pretty sure at this point date two is in the bag. For that very reason, it's probably a good idea to end the date sooner rather than later, on a high note. What could be more alluring than leaving him wanting more?

If you carry on, particularly if you're out drinking, there is far more scope for things to degenerate. I did say in the introduction to this book that I am not here to dictate if and when you should sleep with your dates. Quite frankly, it's nobody's business but yours. But I will say this: If he never calls you, you'll feel a whole lot better if you didn't have sex with him.

CHAPTER 8

Feeling
Hot, Hot, Hot!

If you feel fabulous on the outside you're going to feel fabulous on the inside which will supercharge your confidence, help you feel more at ease and make for an altogether more enjoyable date – for both of you (even guys can pick up on bad-hair-day vibes).

The good news is you don't need Kate Moss's wardrobe, Myleene Klass's body or Cheryl Cole's face to look fabulous. Hurrah! The bad news is that if my own experiences are anything to go by, you will probably wake up on the day of the date having a bad hair day or a 'fat' day, or with a volcanic zit on your nose (it's sod's law). But, that's okay because bad hair can be disguised, zits can be concealed and the fat day is all in your head, anyway.

Preparation is key

Now, I'm not suggesting you blow a fortune on designer clothes and spend three weeks eating cabbage soup in preparation for your debut. You're going to the pub, not the Oscars. Besides, if things do go well, he's going to see you first thing in the morning with no make-up on at some point, so you don't want to blow it with false advertising. Having said that, a little advance preparation and forethought can go a long way.

Let me be a horrible warning #7: Leave enough time to get ready

Do NOT follow this ten-step technique. I have been using it for many years and I promise you it always ends in disaster. You don't want to turn up to the date crying now, do you?

1. Wake up in a blind panic having left all tanning/waxing/plucking/nail-painting to the day of the date.

2. Establish that you have nothing in your wardrobe that's clean/flattering/hole-free and resolve to purchase a fabulous new wow-factor dress in your lunch hour.

3. Run from shop to shop in your break getting hotter, sweatier and closer to tears as you try on a plethora of unsuitable ill-fitting garments, one of which you will inevitably get stuck in (they only had a size 8 left and you were getting desperate) and will have to have rolled over your head like a reverse-condom manoeuvre by the sneering sales assistant.

4. Spend the afternoon at work mentally trying on every possible outfit combination in your wardrobe to save time when you get in.

5. Get home and try on every possible outfit combination in your wardrobe having not saved any time by mentally doing this earlier in the day. NB: Be sure to chuck everything all over your room.

6. Try on everything once more, unable to locate priority items amid the mess, and decide on an outfit that you know is really boring but makes you feel the least fat.

7. Take five minutes (you are so late it's not funny) to shower, wash and condition your hair, shave your legs, wax your bikini line and pluck your eyebrows.

8. Decide your outfit is too boring and go for the slightly trendier one that makes your thighs look a bit big.

9. Apply make-up three times as it keeps sliding off your hot, sweaty skin.

10. Realise the trendier/less-flattering outfit is too creased after being chucked across your room and that ironing boards are out of the question at this stage so revert to outfit one.

It's not what you wear it's the way that you wear it

Whenever I'm having an 'I hate all my clothes!' crisis these days (about twice a week), I try to imagine what each outfit would look like if my friend Sam were wearing it. Sam is one of those girls who oozes cool and sex appeal. That friend you'd love to hate, except you can't because she's so damn lovely. You know the one who breezes through life being effortlessly good at everything and looking fabulous in the process – even while covered in mud on a mountain bike. She could make tripping over a paving stone look like an applaud-inducing move from *Strictly Come Dancing* and looks better in jeans and an old T-shirt than most of us could hope to look in head-to-toe Marc Jacobs. She's one of those girls who can transform a bad hair day in a nano-second with a flick of the wrist and a biro to hold it in place. I have spent years trying to master this trick and always end up looking like I've had a fight in a stationery cupboard. And lost.

So Sam is drop-dead gorgeous and naturally skinny, right? Wrong! Sometimes she gets spots, one of her teeth is a little bit crooked and she has a slightly sticky-out tummy. In other words, she is 'normal'. But Sam holds the secret – a must-have 'it' accessory that never goes out of fashion and makes every item in your wardrobe look a million dollars: Confidence. She doesn't spend hours in front of the mirror questioning whether this top is trendy enough or those jeans make her bum look big, she just asks herself if she likes this top/that pair of jeans and if the answer's yes, that's good enough for her. And as a result whatever she wears you find yourself wanting to go out and buy one – even if it's a white vest from Primark.

So, next time you're stressing about your clothes, ask yourself this: What is the real problem here, the outfit or you? If the answer is the latter, look in the mirror, throw your shoulders back, flash your biggest smile, say, 'I'm fabulous' and be on your way. Failing that, invest in a pair of bright red killer heels and the confidence will follow.

Do guys really care, anyway?

Guys are simple creatures. They notice things like eyes and hair and boobs and bums . . . They'll probably notice if you've gone to the trouble of putting on a frock or you're wearing a sexy top. They might even notice a pair of four-inch heels. But, unless you're going out with one of those uber-trendy types (easily identifiable by a statement fringe and well-kept trainers), your date is not going to know his Prada from his Peacock's. Nor is he likely to care. I read a magazine article a few years ago where a girl was sent on three dates with three different men, and each time she went to the bathroom she had to change something she was wearing to see if he would notice. One of the dates cottoned on pretty quickly and noticed she had changed her necklace immediately. One of them only noticed, after three outfit changes, as they were paying the bill. And the other had absolutely no idea until he was told at the end of the night. So, chill out, you're not going on a date with Gok Wan. Although if, like me, you do go for those cool-trainers types, you have permission to panic and go shopping immediately.

Fashion figure-fixes

If my friends are anything to go by, 'huge bums' and 'stumpy legs' are usually in the eye of the beholder and to anyone else look perfectly normal. But self-esteem starts in the mirror so if you want to overcome your self-esteem stumbling blocks before the date, here are a few ways to cheat.

Body bugbear: Short legs
Banish it: Skinny jeans with heels will make legs look longer and leaner. High-waisted jeans will also add length, but if you're too self-conscious about your tummy try cinching in your top with a wide belt high on the waist.

Body bugbear: Big bum
Banish it: Bootylicious ladies often go for longer tops to hide their behinds, but anything that clings over jeans will add bulk and have the opposite effect. Tunic tops and smock-style dresses over tights or leggings will create a leaner silhouette.

Body bugbear: Round stomach
Banish it: Disguise a sticking-out tum by going for tops that are fitted at the top and then float away from the body from an empire-line seam that sits just under the chest. Blazers are also great for disguising your stomach and creating the impression of a slimmer waist.

Body bugbear: Big hips
Banish it: If you're slim at the top and bigger from the waist down, take attention away from the hips and balance out your figure by going for a statement necklace or a bold print top, with a plain dark skirt or trousers at the bottom. Tops with horizontal stripes are great for balancing width at the bottom.

Dating diva DOs and DON'Ts

DO go for less is more

No, I don't mean turn up in a bikini. I'm talking about over-accessorising here. You don't want to give the poor guy sensory overload. He's there to see you, not the entire contents of your wardrobe. Plus the more accoutrements you have dangling from your person, the more chance there is of having a 'fashion accident'. Chandelier earrings falling into cleavages, scarves dipping into dinners, bracelets laddering tights . . . the possibilities are endless.

DON'T try too hard

Is it just me, or does it always seem to be those spontaneous nights when you've gone out straight from work wearing your least favourite outfit – and haven't bothered washing your hair – when you get the most male attention? Now, I'm not suggesting you turn up to the date looking like a bag lady, he'll appreciate you making an effort, but ultimately it's the real you underneath the slap and super-trendy outfit he's going to fall for (the smile, the twinkle in the eye, the freckles . . .). Relax and think effortless glamour.

DO dress according to the occasion

You might look absolutely spectacular in the dress you wore for your cousin's wedding, but you are going to look spectacularly silly if you turn up wearing it down the Dog & Duck for Sunday lunch. Equally, your leg-lengthening wedge-heels won't look so leg lengthening when they're wedged into the mud on a country ramble. Get the picture? If you're not sure about the dress code of where you're going, do a little bit of research and find out.

DON'T get your haircut the day before a date

I don't care if you've been going to Miguel for ten years and he's never messed up a hair on your head. There's a first time for everything and Miguel's first off-day will most definitely be the day before your first date.

Let me be a horrible warning #8:
Don't cut your fringe on the way to the date

The same goes for any DIY styling experiments. A few months ago I made the mistake of attempting an emergency pre-date fringe-trim. Unfortunately, with only seconds to perform the task before catching my train and only a large pair of plastic-handled stationery scissors to hand, disaster was inevitable. The fringe, of course, was completely crooked forcing me to finish off the job while standing up on a packed moving train using a tiny hand-held mirror much to the amusement/ horror of fellow commuters. By the time I arrived the fringe was so short I was practically receding. When my bemused date enquired about the large amount of hair all over my face (there was now more on the lower half of my face than my forehead), I was forced to 'fess up about the debacle, red (and hairy) faced.

DO think about the height/heels issue

If he is 5'9" and you're 5'7", it doesn't take Einstein to work out that if you go out in four-inch heels you are going to become two inches taller than him. Now, I don't mean to sound sexist here – one of my male

121

friends is getting married to a lovely lady three inches taller than him and I've never seen a more besotted couple, while another close girl friend has a real thing for short guys. But if, like me, you do find the idea of towering above him a turn-off (and he might well do as guys do like to feel kinda manly), then bear this in mind and go for the ballet flats if necessary.

DON'T try to be someone else

Now is not the time to have an identity crisis and start experimenting with a brand new you. You're the girl he's chosen to meet up with. If you're not a skinny jeans kind of a girl, don't wear skinny jeans. If he only likes girls who wear skinny jeans, you're not the girl for him and he's not the man for you. Be honest with yourself, and him, about who you really are. You can only pretend for so long. And don't forget, you have a pretty cool personal style yourself so work it.

DO choose your outfit in advance

. . . and stick to it. Don't try anything else on 'just to be sure' at the last minute. Trust your judgment. If it looked good two days ago it will look good today – even if you did eat that third Krispy Kreme this afternoon.

When you've tried on every outfit combination ten times, things can start to blur into one. This is when it's a good idea to enlist the help of a friend. Ideally, a trusted one who will tell you if she thinks you look silly – even better, a male friend who can give you the man's perspective.

DON'T wear anything too revealing

You don't need to look sexually provocative to look sexy. In fact, most men would agree that it's way sexier to leave something to the imagination. If your boobs are spilling out of your top he will no doubt spend most of the evening concentrating on not looking at or thinking about your boobs . . . and the other bit looking at them and thinking about them. You don't want your date to think he's onto a surefire winner, you want to keep him guessing.

DO make sure it's clean and ironed

If you forgot to put your favourite top in the wash and it's a bit whiffy under the arms, don't believe for a second that a spritz of perfume is going to help. At best you will smell like you've put too much perfume on. At worst, you'll smell of Eau de BO. Go for another top that's clean. I'll do anything to avoid ironing but this is one occasion I will make the effort because a creased top will tell him he just wasn't worth the effort. Let's not even go there with stains.

DON'T fake tan or wax on the day

There are few things more likely to turn him off than streaky orange skin or a bright red 'tache rash. The problem with beauty procedures is that you generally have to look a lot worse in order to look a lot better. The transformation from 'before' to 'after' may well be stunning but the 'during' is never pretty. Unless you fake tan every day and know exactly what you're doing don't risk applying it on the day. I've never heard of a girl failing to make it to a second date because her skin was too pale.

DO love your body

Thinking positively about your body will immediately improve your posture and supercharge your sex appeal.

'The sexiest girl I've ever been on date with was a little bit overweight. I'm not talking morbidly obese, but she was definitely carrying a few extra pounds. But boy did she know how to carry them! She walked like a supermodel and had a smile that left me speechless. I spent the entire night thinking about kissing her. She didn't let me until date three . . . but it was well worth the wait!' Simon, 25, Bradford

DON'T wear new shoes

Those four-inch stilettos may well be sex-on-legs, but on your unaccustomed feet they are going to be hell-on-earth by the time you arrive at the date. Heaven forbid he suggests you move on to that great little boozer he knows, just a ten-minute walk away. Forget sashaying down the street, femme fatale style. You will more likely be hobbling, wincing and bleeding.

DO indulge in some pre-date pampering

Unless you're going out straight from work, set aside some 'me' time for a DIY home-spa to relax your mind and body and make you feel super-sexy. Run a hot bath, exfoliate and moisturise your skin, deep-condition your hair, and most importantly, take it easy. When you arrive at the date you'll be feeling calm and emanating that just-spent-a-week-at-a-spa-retreat glow.

First-date fabulous beauty tips

Wide-eyed beauty

I asked lots of men what's the first thing they notice about a girl on a date and the most popular answer by far was eyes. If you want to make yours appear bigger, dab white eyeshadow at the inner corners and use eyeliner along the upper lashes only. Black liquid liner flicked out at the edges is the perfect sex-kitten look.

Don't even think about attempting false lashes. One of them is bound to start escaping mid-date. For really full lashes that don't look 'cakey', curl lashes with a lash curler then apply two coats of volumising mascara, separating lashes with a comb after each coat is dry.

Kissable lips

Forget collagen injections – wake up with a plumper super-soft pout on the morning of the date by brushing your lips gently with an old toothbrush and slathering with lots of Vaseline or lip balm before you go to bed. Too much lipstick can look harsh and unflattering. For lips that look as though they are naturally bursting with colour, try rubbing your finger over your lipstick and pressing the colour into your lips. For a more girlie touch, finish with a slick of clear gloss.

To avoid the old lipstick-on-teeth blunder, put your finger into your mouth, close your lips around it and slide it back out again.

Zit-zapper

Don't be tempted to start prodding and squeezing a spot before the date or you could end up with a disaster on your hands . . . your face. Instead, dab with concealer after you've applied your foundation and then gently press with powder to take away the oily sheen and prevent it catching the light. Remember that spots always look magnified to you. He probably won't even notice – especially if you choose a nice dimly lit bar!

Sexy scent

A spritz of scent can be very seductive, but too much perfume is worse than no perfume at all so never go for that 'one more for luck' spray. Don't forget that your nose has become accustomed to the fragrance so it will seem a lot stronger to others. For a sheer veil of subtle fragrance, spray your scent in the air and then walk through the mist allowing it to fall over your skin. If it's a daytime date, stick to something that's light and fresh or a scented body lotion.

Tan-talising skin

Contrary to what the name suggests, fake tan should not under any circumstances look fake. Here's how to avoid the telltale signs and cheat your golden glow convincingly.

The fake faux-pas: Orange

Avoid it: Unless you are naturally dark or olive-skinned, a deep tan will leave you looking more orange than an Oompa Loompa. For a golden glow, choose the lightest shade and layer it. You can always use a dusting of bronzer on the parts of the skin the sun would naturally kiss (nose, forehead, chin, cheekbones and chest) to boost the colour more naturally.

The fake faux-pas: Streaky

Avoid it: The key to an even streak-free tan lies in the preparation. No amount of blending will help if your skin's texture is uneven underneath. For a silky finish, exfoliate your skin first with a body scrub to remove any coarse dead skin, then slather all over with a rich body lotion. Now your tan should glide on smoothly and effortlessly.

The fake faux-pas: Tanned palms and orange brows

Avoid it: No amount of time in the sun will give you tanned palms, so don't let yourself down at the last hurdle. Once you've applied your tan, wash your hands thoroughly then apply a little to the backs of your hands using a cotton wool pad. Dampen another cotton wool pad with a few drops of water and use to remove any tan from your eyebrows and the base of your heels.

CHAPTER 9
Talk The Talk

Email, text, chat, 'wall posts', Twitter . . . there are so many ways to communicate these days without having to open your mouth, it's amazing anyone can remember how to converse at the best of times, let alone on a first date when even the wittiest wordsmith can be rendered mute (or worse, reduced to a gibbering wreck). Yep, when it comes to paralysing your power of speech first dates are up there with job interviews, dumping your boyfriend and boardroom presentations.

Mute v motor-mouth?

I used to overcompensate for potential awkward silences on first dates by talking faster than a speeding bullet, without drawing breath. Not because I had the foresight to cleverly prepare a number of topics on which to wow my companion and open up lively and entertaining debate. Oh no, this was an involuntary outpouring of largely unconnected sentences that would spew from my mouth like sewage from a pipe – and contain a similar concentration of sh*t (think: 'I have Irritable Bowel Syndrome. Do you have any embarrassing medical conditions?').

That was unless I actually fancied the guy. Then it was worse. I'd assume the look (and IQ) of a rabbit caught before headlights. My face would freeze into an expression of abject panic, my brain take a hike and my mouth simply cease to function. The only thing I could do was blink. And panic. He'd ask, 'What would you like to drink?' and I'd behave as though Chris Tarrant had just asked me the million-dollar question on *Who Wants To Be A Millionaire* ('Er, can I phone a friend, please?').

But fortunately, thanks to my fair share of dating practice over the years, I reached a point some time ago when I actually started to thrive on the thrill of that first-date banter. Give or take the odd meltdown, of course. Here are a few of the tips I've picked up along the way.

Breaking the ice

You might think this is going to be the scariest part of the date, but in some ways it's often the easiest because firstly, you haven't used up any of your conversation topics yet and secondly, you've got all that greeting stuff to get you through the first few minutes. These apparently dull as ditchwater questions are in actual fact first-date life-lines:

'Sorry I'm late. How long have you been waiting?'

'How did you get here?'

'How long did it take you? Where have you come in from?'

'The traffic was a nightmare today. Do you drive?'

'Did you see that police car up the road? What do you reckon all that was about?'

'What can I get you to drink?'

'Have you been to this place before?'

'It's absolutely freezing out there. Do you think this summer's ever going to start?'

Who cares about the weather? This is simply a cover while you both absorb all that essential first impression stuff. You might be talking about buses, traffic, weather but really all you're both thinking is eyes, height, shoes . . .

An exercise in small talk
If even the thought of small-talk seems daunting, try this simple exercise prior to your date: Next time you're meeting a friend for lunch or at the pub, take a mental note of how the conversation starts. You can do the same trick when you're out and about by earwigging on other people's opening conversations. Try not to get caught though, dictaphones are not advisable!

Be honest about your nerves
No matter how cool, calm and collected your date may

appear, underneath he will be a bag of nerves. That much I can guarantee. By being honest about your own nerves, it will immediately make him feel more at ease – even if he won't admit it. It will also cut through any stiff formality and put you on a more personal and intimate level with one another. He will respect you for your honesty and probably find your vulnerability super-sexy. Don't go into too much detail though. He doesn't need to know you've spent half the morning on the loo. Try a simple 'I actually felt a bit nervous on the way here. Funny things, dates, aren't they?' Cue lots of silly stories about past dates. Bingo!

Laughter is the best medicine

Nothing relieves tension faster than a good chuckle so keep your eyes and ears open on your way to the date for any amusing characters or conversations you come across or scan the bar for any comedy material. I went on a date in a pub over Christmas where they had the creepiest looking illuminated one-eyed reindeer that seemed to swivel its head in our direction every time one of us spoke. We spent the first five minutes of the date laughing so hard we didn't even need to speak.

Ice 'breaker'?

'I was so nervous before my first date with Rob* I took complete leave of my senses – particularly my eyesight. I walked around the pub three times unable to find the door, which in my defence was cunningly disguised as part of the wall thanks to loads of music posters. I found it eventually though, but only when I stopped right outside

it and someone walked out, smacking me straight in the face with it. Rob witnessed the entire episode and was in hysterics when I walked in. Aside from the blossoming black eye, this was the best thing that could have happened for our date. It kept us talking for at least the first 20 minutes and every time we did get an awkward silence we'd just burst out laughing again. It also gave Rob a great excuse to touch my face. We've been married for nearly two years now.' Caroline, 26, Nottingham

Listening and interrupting:
Two conversation myths busted

MYTH: 'You have two ears and one mouth for a good reason.'

TRUTH (according to Cosmo's dating gospel): 'It's not how much you're listening, it's how well you're listening.'

Some experts reckon that for a successful conversation you should spend twice as much time listening as you do talking (hence the phrase). Personally, I would be very wary of trying this on a first date. Just think if he has the same idea you'll end up spending two thirds of the conversation in embarrassed silence, listening to each other breathing. That would just be weird. So next time someone says to you, 'you've got two ears and one mouth for a very good reason', just retort with, 'Yeah, one mouth for talking and two ears for my iPod headphones.'

The most important thing is that your conversation is natural, relaxed and intuitive so forget fretting about whether you're over or under your listening quota for the evening and focus on tuning in to the flow of the chat and where it's headed.

If you've just asked a question then of course you should be listening. Asking a question and ignoring the answer is one of the biggest conversation crimes you could commit on a first date. But that said if your date seems to be floundering with his response, don't just sit there and watch him squirm. Step in and help. Rephrase the question if necessary or move the subject on ('Oh look over there, that woman's got loo paper stuck to her shoe', that kind of thing).

MYTH: 'It's rude to interrupt.'

TRUTH (according to Cosmo's dating gospel): 'Butt in, but know when to do it.'

Talking over the top of someone is a sure-fire way to come across as rude, arrogant and aggressive. But in fact interrupting in a one-on-one situation can also indicate that you are listening, reacting and responding to what the other person is saying.

Which would you find more disconcerting if you were telling a story on a date? The person who keeps chipping in with comments at every step of the way, or the person who stares blankly at you showing no signs of what they are thinking?

Let's face it, neither sounds like a particularly enjoyable way to spend an evening. So how do you get the balance right? How can you appear interested and contribute to the flow of the chat without stampeding your way through the date like a bull in a china shop?

It's all in the timing. Listen carefully to what the other person is saying. If you have something relevant to say in response to his thoughts, wait for a convenient pause in his speech then pounce. But remember you're joining in, not taking over, so never raise your voice above his. This is the conversational equivalent of elbowing your way in front of someone in a queue. Try to be inclusive. A good trick is to establish eye contact, lean in closer and lower your voice. This conspiratorial move will make your date feel that he is still in control of the conversation and bag you tons of brownie points to boot.

'Enough about me, what about you?'

So you've got the art of listening down to a tee. In fact, you're kind of hoping he never shuts up so you can continue to nod, smile, laugh, sip your drink and look pretty for the rest of the evening. But, sadly you know that's not an option. Any second now he's going to finish telling you about his three-day charity hike up Kilimanjaro and utter those dreaded words, 'So, enough about me. What do *you* get excited about?' The trouble is, the only things that are springing to mind right now are last night's cliff-hanger on *Corrie*, your new dress from H&M ('You can imagine my excitement when I saw the price tag. I mean £12!') and yesterday's supermarket revelation ('It tastes just like cheesecake, but get this – it's yogurt . . . and it's *fat free*!').

Actually, there's nothing wrong with discussing the merits of fat-free cheesecake yogurt. In fact, food is a good leveller when the conversation seems to going off in a direction you're not comfortable with. After all, we all eat. But the point is when you're under pressure – and it doesn't get more high-pressured than on a first-date – it can be all too easy to go into meltdown. The gregarious, hilarious girl all your friends know and love – and the one that charmed your date over email – has apparently stood you up. Suddenly, you feel as though you've had a sense of humour bypass and developed amnesia with regard to anything interesting or funny that you've ever done or said in your entire life.

This can be completely confidence crushing and the more you become aware of it the more magnified the feeling. Yet this has absolutely nothing to do with your natural ability to communicate and entertain or how fantastic you are as a person. It is down to one thing and one thing only: Nerves.

So what are you going to do about it? If you find yourself feeling a tad overwhelmed by the whole conversation thing, it might help to break things down. There are essentially four ways you can communicate with conversation:

The Four As:
- Asking
- Answering
- Anecdotes
- Analysing

Asking
Asking your date lots of questions will not only take the pressure off you, but it will also help you to get to know

him better. Learning about his interests and aspirations will help you to find common links and give you new leads for potential conversation topics. It will also demonstrate that you're genuinely interested in him, which should in turn put him at his ease and bolster his confidence. Plus, there is nothing more off-putting than an ego-maniac who talks about nothing but herself.

Don't fire too many questions though. This is a date not an interrogation. Remember the guy is under just as much pressure as you, so give him a break. Choose topics you know he'll feel comfortable talking about like his interests, or what he got up to at work that day, or something you've previously chatted about on email. Leave the challenging stuff for a later date . . . or when he's had a couple of drinks. After all, most men know all the answers to all life's great mysteries after a few beers.

To keep the conversation flowing, avoid asking closed questions where he can get away with a yes or no answer. Instead of 'Did you have a busy day at work today?' say 'What was the highlight of your day today?' It's not rocket science but it's surprising how easy it can be to forget the simple stuff once the nerves kick in. Try thinking up a few questions on the way there to get you into the right mode of thinking.

Answering

This is the part of every date I fear the most: The spot-light. What if he asks me a current affairs question and I don't know the answer? What if he asks me if I drive (I am the only 34 year old on the planet who can't)? What if he asks me if I've been skiing (I am the only 34 year old on the planet who hasn't)? What if he asks me what I did last night and I accidentally tell him the truth (a Brazilian bikini wax)?

I'm a music geek who eats books for breakfast and goes to the cinema at least once a week, yet faced with a question about the last CD I bought/book I read/film I watched in a date scenario my mind goes completely blank. Heaven forbid anyone should invite me to a pub quiz for a first-date. Facing questions from my date and a quiz-host simultaneously would probably bring on some kind of brain seizure.

Although I still have a deep-seated fear of questions, the situation improved greatly when I realised that I was focused on being the person the date would want me to be and not the person I really am. Now, instead of giving the answer I think will impress my date, I just give the honest answer (the one I would have to if all my mates were standing behind me, listening). I always go with a book/film/CD in mind, too – just in case.

This is your opportunity to get a bit of lively banter going, so don't give monosyllabic one-word answers even if he does keep asking you yes or no questions. If he asks, 'Do you like going to the cinema?' don't just say yes. Tell him about a film you've seen recently that you feel strongly about, whether it's something you loved or hated, and bounce a question back to him. Ask him if he's seen the film and what he thought about it, and if not what has he seen lately that has provoked a reaction. Before you know it the conversation will have gone off on a tangent about something completely unexpected, which is always a very good sign on a date. It means you're no longer thinking about the fact you're on a date – you're actually getting on.

Anecdotes

Never underestimate the power of a good story. Most of us seek them out on a daily basis without even realising it. Does this day sound familiar to you? You get up, catch a bit of the breakfast news on TV, read a paper on the way to work, get the lowdown on last night's gossip when you arrive at the office, flick through a magazine at lunchtime to get your fix of celebrity gossip, get home, switch on the TV for the daily round of soaps and dramas or maybe go out to the cinema then fall asleep with a good book. From global news to celebrity misbehaviour to your mates' latest shenanigans, it's in our nature to be intrigued by the stories, lives and actions of others, however trivial. So if you really want to reel him in and have him hooked for the evening you can't go far wrong with a few choice anecdotes.

'But I'm no good at telling stories!'

Luckily, you don't need to have the gift of the gab to be able to relay a good yarn. In fact, it's more important to know when to shut up. The shorter the tale, the easier it will be to hold his interest.

The key to being an ace raconteur is to stick to the point. Here's a good example of how *not* to: 'Oh, this funny thing happened to me on Tuesday . . . hmm, or was it Wednesday . . . no, it can't have been Wednesday, I was at the doctor's on Wednesday . . . no, I tell a lie it was Thursday . . . it must have been Thursday, yes, that's right, because I took the car to the garage on Thursday . . . ' Who cares when it was or when you went to the doctor's? Make up the day, just get to the point!

'I don't have any interesting stories to tell'
One of the most entertaining stories I've ever heard on a date was about a funny incident that happened on someone's bus journey to work, while undoubtedly the most boring was about a three-day jungle adventure in Borneo. The point is, you don't need to have led the most exotic or adventurous life in order to tell a fantastic tale, you just need to be observant about the little things that happen in day-to-day life, however big or small. The best stories have a surprising, shocking or funny element and are the kind the listener can identify with or relate to. For inspiration, ask yourself the following questions:

When was the last time you did something embarrassing?

What was the most interesting thing that happened at work this week?

What was the naughtiest thing you did when you were little?

What's the funniest thing that's ever happened to you on a date?

What's the scariest thing you've ever done?

What's the funniest story any of your friends have ever told you?

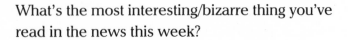

What's the most interesting/bizarre thing you've read in the news this week?

Analysing

It's a sure sign the date is going well when the chat goes off on a complete tangent. You know the one, you start off talking about the weather and before you know it three hours has passed and you've covered everything from the ridiculous to the sublime. From the person you'd least like to be stuck in a lift with, to why the word lisp has an 's' in it, to how to make perfect lump-free mash, the best banter is based around analysing, musing and philosophising.

This is not as intellectually highbrow or dry as it might sound. We're not talking about solving life's great mysteries here, or trying to work out the meaning of life, but rather musing on the minutiae of the everyday. Even your thoughts on last night's *Big Brother* eviction decision can make a great starting point for a random, thought-provoking chat. But be warned, these chats have a tendency to take you through several glasses of wine and into the wee small hours.

'Rick and I realised at the end of our first date that we'd barely learned a thing about each other in terms of the usual stuff. Neither of us had talked about our jobs or our families or what we like to do at the weekends. Instead, mesmerised by the eccentric-looking landlord and landlady behind the bar, we had spent the entire evening analysing them and making up stories for them. We gave them names, decided how they met, how long they'd been together, what they got up to

when they weren't behind the bar . . . it was way more fun than the usual small talk. We even went back there for our one-year anniversary and were delighted to see "Elvis and Ethel" were still there!' Jane, 30, Aberystwyth

Well, what can I say?

Lost for words? You can't go wrong with one of these awkward-silence savers.

Work
It might not sound very sexy but it's one thing we all have in common. From the worst job you've ever had to the dream career you're working towards, there's plenty of scope for interesting chat, but don't go into too much detail – 'spreadsheet' is not a word anyone wants to hear on a first date.

Interests
If he's passionate about something, the chances are he'll love to talk about it. He'll want to know about your interests too. If they only amount to shopping and drinking, it might be time to think about broadening your horizons and getting out more.

What's around you
Use the environment around you on the date to inspire spontaneous banter – whether it's the cool view from the window, the conversation you just overheard at the bar or even the drunk guy in the corner of the pub who just walked into a table.

Films, books, TV, music . . .
Great if you like the same films/books/music, great if you don't – either way you've got a brilliant starting point for a discussion. Having polar opposite tastes is not necessarily a bad thing as long as you can agree to disagree. Slanging matches are never a good start.

News
It's probably wise to keep heavy political debate off the agenda; the guy's on a date, not Question Time. There is plenty of time for full-blown arguments further down the line. For now, stick to funny, bizarre or heart-warming news snippets.

Food
You know what they say, a way to a man's heart is through his stomach. Show me a man who wouldn't marry Nigella Lawson. And thanks to Jamie Oliver and Gordon Ramsay et al, blokes are finally getting into the kitchen, too. Who'd have thought recipes could make for sexy date talk.

Travels
Swapping stories about the far-flung places you've visited is always fun, particularly if you've travelled the same path. But do bear in mind that a blow-by-blow account of someone else's exotic adventure is about as exciting as trawling through someone else's holiday snaps – that is, not exciting at all.

Nostalgia

Discussing the virtues of *The Magic Roundabout* and Cola Cubes has become a bit of a cliché these days, but reminiscing about a shared history is a great way to bond. Most of us have plenty of horror stories to regale about our childhoods, from evil teachers to dodgy fashion faux pas. Avoid this subject if there's a huge age gap between you. If you were five when he was 15, don't even go there.

Friends and family

You can learn a lot about a man by his relationship to his friends and family. If he talks fondly about his best mates, parents and siblings, it suggests he's loyal and caring. If he spends the date regaling stories about nights out with Bazza, Dazza, Gazza, beware the LAD.

You know it's time to shout 'Taxi!' when he says . . .

'But you really remind me of my ex girlfriend . . .'

'Oh no, this is really embarrassing but I seem to have forgotten my wallet.'

'Well, when we broke up it was so amicable, we didn't see the point in one of us moving out so I just moved into the spare room. Would you like to come back for a coffee?'

'Now I've brought a couple of surprise guests along. They were dying to meet you. Mum, dad, this is . . .'

'I hope you don't mind me choosing a pub with a big screen. I never miss a match.'

'I hate to tell you this but I thought you should know you have a massive bogey hanging out of your nose.'

'There's a Scientology meeting on this afternoon. I really think you should come along.'

'You looked a lot slimmer in your profile picture. Was it taken a while ago?'

'No, I wasn't at a wedding in that picture. I always wear this top hat. "Top-hat Tom" they call me.'

'Don't look now but my ex has just walked in.'

'. . . then we got to Borneo and began the three day trek through . . . hey, how about you come to mine and I'll show you the pictures. There are only 987.'

'I can't see the band properly, would you mind if I sat on your shoulders? Oh to be tall, like you.'

'Another drink? Nah, I think we both know what we're here for, let's just get a cab back to mine.'

'When I lose my virginity I want it to be on my honeymoon with the woman I'm going to spend the rest of my life with.'

'So, I do know of a great party on down the road. Have you ever been to a swingers' party?'

10 First-date dialogue DON'Ts

1. DON'T exaggerate or lie about anything. It will catch up with you.

2. DON'T get on your soapbox. Nobody loves a whinger.

3. DON'T make inappropriate jokes. Leave your dark sense of humour at home.

4. DON'T be too dogmatic in your opinions. This shouts arrogance.

5. DON'T stare at the hot man who just walked through the door. D'uh!

6. DON'T talk about yourself continuously. He will get bored.

7. DON'T pry into his personal life. This is not the time to ask about his ex.

8. DON'T show off to impress him. He'll think you're sad.

9. DON'T reveal your dark side. He doesn't need to know about the PMT and 'white wine witch syndrome' . . . yet.

10. DON'T talk about shoes and shopping. Unless he brings them up.

CHAPTER 10

The Way You Move

Okay, so you've got the killer outfit and the chat sorted. Now it's time to wheel out your most powerful seduction tool of all – your body. I'm not suggesting you pop on a pair of nipple tassels and offer yourself to him on a plate. We're talking body language here; the subtle moves that will have him fall under your spell before he can say, 'what would you like to drink?'

Experts reckon that we decide if we fancy someone within the first five minutes of meeting them. They also claim that the majority of that all-important first impression comes from our body language. So, you do the maths – if you want him to stick around, you've got to get your moves in fast.

Your appearance, posture and the way you move gives away far more about your personality than you might realise. But if his body's doing the talking, what the hell is it trying to say and how do you respond with the right signals?

The art of silent flirting

The triangle
When we look at people we don't know we naturally move our eyes in a zig-zag motion, from eye to eye and across the bridge of the nose. With friends we move them in a triangle, also looking down at the nose and mouth. If we're attracted to the person we're looking at the triangle gets wider at the bottom as we look further down and incorporate their body into our gaze. If he is looking intensely from eye to eye, he is definitely flirting – especially if he is lingering on your mouth, which could be a sign he is wondering what it would be like to kiss you. If he's lingering on your boobs, however, this is probably time to down your drink and make a sharp exit.

The copycat
It's a sure sign of chemistry when you start to mirror one another's moves. Try copying his posture and gestures and he will be seduced without even realising it. If he takes a sip of his drink and looks you in the eye, do the same and meet his gaze. If he leans in to say something, lean in close to meet him.

Body language buffs suggest that by mirroring someone's moves we are demonstrating that we are on the same wavelength as them. Don't take the mirroring phrase too literally though. If you try and copy their exact moves at the same time as them, they will probably feel slightly freaked out or as though you are taking the Mickey.

The eyebrow raiser

The first thing we often do as a sign of greeting when we see someone we know is raise our eyebrows. But while the gesture usually only lasts a fraction of a second, it is prolonged when we are attracted to someone. If they feel the same they will do the same in return.

So, if you want to let him know you're interested you could try raising your brow and catching his eye at the same time. Although I suspect this is the kind of move that could go horribly wrong the minute you become conscious of what you're doing. Raise your brows too high or for too long and it will look like you've just graduated from the Carry On school of flirting – either that or you'll just look shocked. And nobody wants their date's first impression to be shock.

The point

If we find someone attractive, we'll often point a part of our body towards them as a subconscious indication we're interested – and on the same subconscious level, they will probably pick up on this.

I'm not suggesting you outstretch your arms and legs towards him like an amorous zombie – subtlety is the key. All you need to do to make your intentions known is turn your feet or hands towards him, angle your upper body or tilt your head in his direction.

The blink

It's a well-known fact that our pupils get bigger when we're looking at something we like. But did you know we apparently blink faster, too? Without wanting to look as though you have something stuck in your eye, you could try upping your blink rate and see if he does the same.

On the subject of eye contact, holding his gaze is one of the sexiest green-light signals you can give him. But the best way to ship him up into a frenzy of excitement is to build it up gradually. Start by catching his eye then lowering your gaze then begin holding his gaze for longer and teaming it with a hint of a smile.

The hand gesture

Unclenched hands show you're open to him while touching objects such as the rim of your glass can be super-sensual and suggestive. Be careful to use light, caressing strokes as opposed to fidgety moves though. Given that your moves will be indicative of what you'd like to do to him, ripping up your beer mat is probably not a good idea. If the date's going well and you're pretty sure the feeling's mutual, you could even take the plunge and touch him, whether it's touching his arm for a second when you're making a point or agreeing with his, or 'accidentally' brushing his hand or his knee with yours.

The girlie tactics

Ever noticed that when women are flirting they tend to come over all bashful and girlie? It's a natural instinct to bring out your feminine wiles when on a full-on charm offensive and it usually gets a positive response. Slightly tilting your head, twiddling your hair, biting your lower lip and lowering your head so you're looking up at him coyly are all tricks we are programmed to use when we want to get our own way and play on our powers of persuasion. Don't go overboard though, sucking your thumb is definitely over-stepping the mark.

To kiss or not to kiss

Q: *I know this sounds stupid but what are you supposed to do when you greet someone on a date? Do you shake their hand, give them a peck on the cheek, a peck on both cheeks or not touch them at all? I always feel really awkward and end up getting flustered and going bright red. Not the best way to start a date. Please help!* **Tania, 26, Blackburn**

A: This is a very good question and one that can lead to all manner of awkward situations. For our more tactile European cousins in France and Spain, things are much simpler as they use the same greeting – a kiss on each cheek – whatever the occasion, whether they're in a business meeting, greeting old friends or on a first date. Sadly, in the more reserved UK there is no set rule, so even the most seasoned dater can only account for her own part in the proceedings. There's no knowing which move he is going to make. While you lean in for a kiss, he could hold out his hand for a handshake. It's a bit like playing 'paper, scissors, rock'.

To minimise the chances of nose bashing, head banging – or worse, that accidental kiss on the lips – I suggest you decide your plan of attack before you walk into the room. A handshake will make him feel as though he has turned up for a job interview, so my

---

advice is to go for the European double kiss. In today's globalised society this has become increasingly accepted in the UK. Move to your left first, then your right and steer well clear of the mouth.

It's also worth bearing in mind that most people touch cheeks while kissing the air, as opposed to planting a smacker. After all, you can't both plant a kiss on the cheek at the same time so that could again lead to an accidental snog if you're not careful.

It could be a bad sign if . . .

He's restless. Fidgeting and shifting in his seat is a sign he doesn't feel comfortable with the situation.

He is looking around the room. If his eyes are roaming everywhere but your direction, his mind is on other things.

His posture is 'closed'. If his posture is stiff and he's crossing his arms, he's on the defensive and doesn't feel open and relaxed.

He is facing away from you. He's subconsciously letting you know that he doesn't want to take things further.

Table manners

Make-up

In old black and white movies the femme fatales make the application of red lipstick look sensual and seductive. Sadly, rummaging through your bag and whipping out a battered plastic lippy in the middle of a crowded restaurant is unlikely to have the same effect. It will look kind of strange. It will look even stranger if you dump your grubby, oversized make-up bag on the table and disappear in a cloud of lipstick, powder and paint between your starter and main. If you need to reapply, excuse yourself and go to the Ladies to 'powder your nose'.

Mobiles

There are few things more annoying when dining out than listening to the loudmouth at the next table shouting down his mobile phone. One of them is listening to your date shouting down his mobile phone right there in front of you. Unless one of you is a doctor on call there should be no mobiles out on the table. Even reading a text message suggests you're not fully engaged with your date and have more interesting things on your mind. If you're absolutely dying to text your friend to tell her he's wearing dodgy shoes, wait until you're in the bathroom.

The Ladies

Having already given license to perform two extra-curricular activities in the Ladies, it might be worth pointing out that by the time you've relieved yourself, reapplied your make-up and texted your best mate about your date's dodgy shoes, he may be wondering if you have climbed out of the toilet window and done a runner. Worse than that, he may suspect some kind of bowel problem. In the case of the latter, a visual will almost certainly have popped into his head. This could turn him off his dinner . . . and you. Hurry up in there!

Coughing and sneezing

Talking of bodily functions, if you have a cold, it is probably worth postponing your first date for a time when you are not coughing, sneezing and sniffling anywhere near him or his plate of food. If you do need to cough or sneeze at any point, I shouldn't need to point out that you must put your hand over your mouth, or if possible use a tissue. I will point out though that your napkin is not a tissue and should not be used as one under any circumstances.

Eating and drinking

Eating with your mouth open is a cardinal sin, as is speaking with your mouth full ('Sorry, I didn't catch that. Could you spray that again?'). Once that food passes your lips that should be the last your date sees of it. If, like me, you have a tendency to inhale your food when you're hungry, make a conscious effort to slow down. Finishing yours while he's still helping himself to greens, and then stealing food off his plate is not very becoming.

Big but: DON'T jump to conclusions

Of course, as body language isn't as direct and literal as the spoken word it's open to all kinds of misunderstanding. He might be pointing his foot away from you because the table's in the way or he's just got cramp; just as he might take your folded arms as a signal you don't fancy him, when in fact you're just trying to hide the fact that the button has just fallen off your top and you don't want him to think you're trying to flash your boobs. For a more accurate interpretation of his feelings towards you, look for several signals that suggest the same thing.

Having said that, I wouldn't get too hung up on body language. For a really successful date I suggest you spend more time listening to what he is saying and less time staring at his feet.

How to lose a man in 10 seconds

Eating with your mouth open

Coughing/sneezing without hand over mouth

Yawning openly while he's talking

Eating with your mouth full/spraying food

Sitting with your legs open (in a skirt!)

Talking 1mm away from his face

Touching his knee (within the first five minutes of the date)

Greeting him with a kiss on the lips

Knocking a bottle of wine over his Paul Smith shirt while 'tipsy'

Flirting with the waiter/barman/glass collector

CHAPTER 11
After The Date

Post-date paranoia

If there's one thing more painful than the aftermath of a disastrous date, it's the aftermath of a brilliant one. At least if you had a *bad* date and didn't fancy him, the grieving process is over before you can say, 'he looked nothing like his picture'. In fact, by the time you've gone home, comfort-eaten the entire contents of your fridge, regaled your flatmate with the low points of the evening over one more glass of wine and had a good night's kip, you're ready to move on and face the next contender.

But the aftermath of a good date – well, that's just bittersweet agony. One minute you're staring into the middle distance with an inane grin on your face as you recount the highlights of the evening (when he accidentally knocked your knee with his; when he said he liked your top; when he looked you straight in the eye for that fraction of a second longer than is usual . . .) the next minute you're gripped with a bout of post-date anxiety (What if he isn't interested? What if he noticed that angry spot? What if he's going on a date with another (spotless) girl from the site tonight?).

Let's face it your anguish is not going to end until you hear from him. But sadly, you have absolutely no idea when that's going to be. Tonight, tomorrow, three days, a week, never . . . Until then you're in post-date purgatory. So what can you do?

Put the thumb down and move away from the phone

It's nobody's business but yours whether or not you make the first move and when you make it. After all, you should just do what feels right. Right? Be yourself . . .

. . . Unless, that is, *your*self is anything like *my*self. In other words, you lose all sense of logic and control of your faculties as soon as you get the slightest inkling you might actually like someone. In which case, you should probably exercise a bit of caution before you reach for your mobile.

Let's put it this way, did you ever hear of a girl getting ditched for *not* making the first move after a date?

Straight after the date: Bask in the afterglow

If you send him a text immediately after the date the content is almost irrelevant. The timing says it all. Even the most easy-breezy of messages will have bunny-boiling undertones in his eyes.

The text: 'Hey, just wanted to say thanks for tonight. I had a great time. X'

The subtext: 'Hey, I fancy you and I want to see you again. Do you fancy me? Do you want to see me again? I can't wait to find out so I'm hoping by sending you this message you'll feel the need to reply immediately and put me out of my misery. That way I know whether to a) stop off on the way home to buy a family bucket of KFC and a bottle of wine to numb the pain of rejection or b) crack on with fantasising about our long and happy future together. Btw, what do you think about the name Jude for a boy? X'

The point is, men do not generally respond well to pressure. The slightest inkling that you might be trying to force the issue or rush things along is likely to have him heading for the hills . . . or the safety of the local boozer with his mates.

Quit thinking about your next move and sit back and enjoy the post-date euphoria while it lasts. If you really can't resist reaching for the phone, call one of your friends instead – ideally the one who's most likely to keep you on the straight and narrow and encourage you to maintain that dignified silence.

The next day: Phone? What phone? I'm far too busy to check my phone . . .

Radio silence the next day is pretty much standard practice, so now is not the time to start worrying. Don't waste your day staring at the phone. There's a very big chance your screen won't light up with his name today. Besides, a watched pot never boils and all that.

Lack of contact at this stage does not mean to say he isn't interested; it doesn't even necessarily mean he's playing it cool. It simply means he's being a bloke. You see unlike us, Average Bloke does not spend the next 24 hours after a date analysing it. That's not to say he's not thinking about you. If he liked you you'll be popping up in his thoughts whenever he gets a spare moment (don't men think about sex every eight seconds or something?). But bear in mind guys are not known for their multi-tasking abilities. They like to deal with one thing at a time. For instance, you're unlikely to be top of his mind when he's in a meeting or trying to figure out what to have for lunch. Likewise, while you're doing a full date-debrief and 'workshopping' your next move with your workmates, he is more likely to be bantering with the lads about the footy results. The chances are he hasn't even told them about your date. Do you have any idea how much grief guys get about these things?

So, my advice is take a leaf out of his book and keep your mind busy with other stuff. The more time you spend obsessing about him now, the greater the disappointment will be if he doesn't call. Arrange a lunch date with a friend, go to the cinema, get your hair cut, kill a few hours on Facebook, read a book . . . just stop thinking about your goddamn mobile.

A week later: Next!

Are you sitting down? Good. I'm afraid I've got some bad news. He's probably not interested. If he was a decent bloke, and into the idea of you and him he would have contacted you by now. In fact he would have been in touch by phone, text or email at least three days ago. But, but, but, what if his computer has broken or he lost his phone? Thanks to the miracle of modern technology, it is practically impossible to *not* be able to get hold of someone these days. It's only a matter of time before I'll have Barack Obama in my Facebook Friends list and a tracking device in my phone to tell me the whereabouts of Brad Pitt at any given moment. The harsh truth is that unless he is clinging to an iceberg in the North Pole, it is very unlikely he has been unable to contact you.

That's not to say he isn't going to change his mind later. He may have met another girl on or off the site at the same time as you and when he realises she is way less cool than you (or she doesn't call him for over a week), he may well be back with renewed vigour and lust, sniffing around for that second date. But right now for whatever reason you are not the girl on his mind. So for the purposes of your sanity, self-respect and future happiness, forget all about this man. What man? That's the spirit.

I suggest you either take a little man-break and revel in the fabulous freedom of singledom for a bit, or get yourself back out there and make contact with some of those other eager dudes on your fans page who will be only too happy to send you a text five minutes after your first date.

Let him down gently in three guilt-free steps

He had an amazing time and can't wait to see you again; you'd rather stay in and de-scale the kettle than spend another evening in his company. So, how do you let him know your first date was also your last?

1. Avoid bad date-karma

Tempting as it might be, don't take the cowardly approach of ignoring his text/email/call, in the hope he'll go away. For one thing he won't go away because in case you'd forgotten you're hanging out on the same dating site. Even if he does leave you in peace, his profile will still be lurking around as a harsh reminder of what a cow you've been.

For another thing, this puts you right in the firing line for some bad date karma. If the next person you go on a date with does exactly the same thing to you, you will not only get a taster of the hurt you've just inflicted, but you'll have absolutely no right to bitch about him (and let's face it, that's the best part of being rejected).

2. Be honest

If you know you never want to see the man again and no amount of new information about him is going to convince you otherwise ('I will grow my beard back'/ 'I have just won the Lottery'/ 'I have a ten-inch willy') you need to make it absolutely clear that a second date is never going to happen. Don't fob him off with half-baked excuses that might give him false hope of a rendezvous further down the line. It's not fair to have him waste his month's subscription chasing you when he could be focusing his attentions on someone who *is* interested. You're going to have to tell him sooner or later, so why prolong the agony? The chances are he'll appreciate your honesty.

3. Not too honest

While it's important to be clear about where the 'relationship' is going (i.e. nowhere), spare him the details and the character assassination. Feeding him the usual 'it's not you, it's me' rubbish might be insulting to his intelligence but it won't be as insulting as telling him his eyes are too close together and he could bore for Britain. Again, think how you would feel in his position.

Sometimes a white lie is the kindest way to bow out, but you need to think very carefully about this if you don't want it to backfire. I was once put on the spot when a date called me from a withheld number to ask me out. Without thinking I replaced the harsh truth 'I don't want to see you again because you're just really irritating' with 'I've decided to get back with my ex'. He was very understanding . . . until he logged on to the site a few hours later to find me back online with a revamped profile and new picture. Oops!

If in doubt, you can't beat the classic, 'you're a lovely guy but I just didn't feel the romantic connection'.

The sex thing

You have a wonderful date, the chemistry is intense, you really fancy him and can't wait to rip his clothes off, he invites you back to his, you spend the night having mind-blowing sex, he even cuddles you for a few minutes before he rolls over and starts snoring, you wake up in his arms, have more amazing morning sex, he kisses you goodbye with promises of calls and second dates, you do the walk of shame home, looking like shit but feeling like you've just won the lottery, then . . . he doesn't call. Ever.

So, are you glad you at least got to have mind-blowing sex with a sexy man, or do you just feel used and humiliated? It's worth asking yourself how you'd react to that scenario before you jump in a cab with him.

The thing is no matter how well you get on, on the date, and how sweet and lovely he is, you don't know the guy. His chivalrous and charming behaviour could be part of his plan to get you between the sheets. Yes, it's cynical, but a little bit of caution at this point could save your self-esteem.

Double standards

'The email banter between Dan and me had been pretty flirtatious and suggestive, and I knew if he was as good looking as his pictures (and the wine was flowing) I'd be tempted to sleep with him. But I promised myself I was going to wait. If he really liked me he'd understand that. Of course, it all went to pot when he turned up looking even more gorgeous than I'd hoped. We immediately clicked. I couldn't believe how many things we had in common. We were both really good friends with the same guy and had come close to meeting numerous times. I could tell he fancied me but he was a lot more shy and sweet than he had been in his emails. There were no innuendos; he just kept telling me that he had a good feeling about us and that there was something very special about me. So when he invited me back to his I was pretty sure he wasn't just after one thing. After chatting for about an hour on the sofa we kissed. It was mind-blowing. And yes, one thing led to another. The sex felt more like lovemaking: slow and intense. I was hooked.

The next day Dan promised he'd text me later that afternoon and true to his word he did. But it wasn't quite the message I'd been hoping for: "Hi Sarah, I had a great time last night but I don't think things would work out for us in the long-term. I'm really sorry." I was gutted. I was even more gutted when I found out through our mutual friend a couple of weeks later that he'd been really put off because I slept with him on the first date!' Sarah, 28, Rugby

The art of multi-dating

One of the advantages of online dating is the volume of choice on offer. What's more you can try as many things on for size as you like before you commit to making a purchase. You're positively encouraged to flirt with and date multiple men without being labelled a two-timing slapper. It's raining men, hallelujah! Of course the downside to this massive flirt-fest is that he's doing exactly the same thing, too. Goddamnit. So how do you manage the situation without turning into a paranoid wreck?

Is it okay to book three first dates in the same week?

When you're still at the emailing stage, it's a good idea to keep your options open. Good email banter does not necessarily mean good chemistry, so don't be so quick to turn down eligible men because you're sure this one is going to be The One. But while there's no harm having irons in a few fires (don't forget he probably has), let's not get carried away. This isn't a competition to score as many dates as you can before your subscription runs out. What with all that pre-date anxiety, the pressure of making small talk (not to mention the pressure on your wallet), the post-date paranoia, and the late-night drinking on a school night, dates can be pretty stressful and exhausting.

Chill out! There's no rush. If you want to make the most of your subscription – and maximise your chances of meeting someone, keep a few email chats on the go but focus on one date at a time.

Do I have a right to ask him if he's seeing anyone else?

It's inevitable that on your first date the subject of online dating will come up in conversation. After all, it's the one thing you're guaranteed to have in common. But while it's okay to swap anecdotes and share your thoughts on the experience as a whole, it's not a good idea at this stage, to start sniffing around trying to find out who else he is seeing. The short story is: He will run a mile. Even if you've been emailing for weeks prior to the date and you feel like you've known each other for years – you don't. You have only just met. No matter how much you're dying to ask, you really need to keep these thoughts to yourself. It may be he has a date booked in the following evening, or that he has already been on a couple of dates with someone he's not sure about. If this is the case, he has still chosen to spend the evening with you. At this point in time, he is still sussing you out, just as you are with him. Leave him to it – he's bound to come running.

I can see he's still going on the site. Can I say something?

Some dating sites, such as The Guardian Soulmates, enable you to see exactly when a person last logged on. But if you know that he is still going on there, you have obviously been on there yourself. So, you're hardly in a position to question him. If you went on to check your emails or browse the latest profiles, you're certainly in no position to judge him. If you only went on to check if he had been on, how are you going to explain that? He'll either think you're a stalker, not believe you or tell you that he only went on for the same reason. So, what exactly are you going to achieve from this? Absolutely nothing.

Until you have been on a few dates and got to know one another properly, try to avoid looking at his movements on the site. If you are right for each other, the chances are it will happen naturally and you will both stop logging on without even realising it. If, a few dates down the line you feel you are ready to start seeing one another exclusively and come off the site, then it's time to lay your cards on the table.

CHAPTER 12

True Stories: The Good, The Bad & The Ugly

Having harassed hundreds of online daters in the name of research for this book everybody has apparently had wildly different experiences. But one piece of advice on which everybody agrees, is always 'expect the un-expected'. From the weird to the wonderful, the horrific to the heart-warming, here are some of the best true-life tales of dating delights and disasters for your delectation.

Lasagne Man

'I saw a guy a few times, who was gorgeous looking (think Damon Albarn), but something about him said "not the commitment type". That was fine by me because I wasn't really ready to jump into a long-term thing either. But I liked him so carried on seeing him. The only problem was I lived with my sister and he lived in a house with a landlady who was very strict about him bringing guests around (apparently). We met several times for meals and

drinks then my sis announced she was going away for the weekend. I told her I would ask Robert* over for some dinner, which she was fine about. Robert phoned me on the night to say his car had broken down, so could I go and get him, so I did, as I had already spent the day slaving over a lasagne and didn't want it to go to waste. I picked him up and brought him to my sis's house. He didn't even have any wine or chocolates, anything, which I thought was a bit rude, but hey. Anyway, we spent a few minutes kissing and cuddling on the sofa, then I said I had better check on the lasagne. On returning from the kitchen, I found Robert with his trousers around his ankles, saying, "let's skip the food and go straight to bed". I have to say I was so offended that I said, "I'll tell you what, let's skip the food and I'll take you straight home". The stupid thing is if he had had the courtesy to eat my food and not make it obvious that he was there for one reason and one reason only, he may have got lucky. But as it was I never saw him again.' Jude, 29, Cornwall

Who's the daddy?

'Steve* and I arranged to meet in a pub but as soon as we arrived, the landlord asked us to join in a pub quiz. I shook my head, but Steve was all for it. Fine, OK, I can do pub quizzes. What I wasn't ready for was answers time. Every time the landlord shouted out an answer that we had got right, Steve shouted out, very loudly, "Who's the daddy!" I was so embarrassed. I never saw him again.' Andrea, 22, Cheltenham

Mr Calculator

'Jon* and I went for a nice curry. I had quite a good evening and he was pretty good looking, although he did go on a bit about himself. But I can be equally guilty sometimes, so I didn't worry too much about that. What did scare me was that at the end of the night, he got his calculator out and worked out how much each of us owed (I owed £3.50 more). I did actually arrange to see him again, but the email before date two which said "I might even kiss you next time" slightly scared me. On the next date, he did the same thing with the calculator. Now I have to add that I am very much up for paying my way and if I am out with friends then I am more than happy to work out the bill, as it is usually me who eats and drinks more, anyway, but there was something slightly off-putting about the calculator coming out, and a friend has never done that, thankfully. I didn't see him again, and he seemed surprised. I even ended up telling him why, as he pestered me a bit. His answer was, "But I thought girls hated being bought".' Carla, 24, Shrewsbury

Just good friends

'I chatted to Alan* for a long time on email (never on the phone). I wasn't sure I would fancy him from his pictures, but I really looked forward to the email banter with him. Eventually we met and he was brilliant, such a lovely person. We had a fab night and to finish it all off, he paid for the meal (not that that really matters, but it does leave you with a good vibe). I saw him again and I offered to pay, but he wouldn't have it. To cut a long

story short, I wasn't really ready to go into a relationship at that time and wasn't bowled over by his looks, and he picked up on that. But we have remained great friends since, and still meet three or four times a year for a drink or dinner. He's now met someone else from the dating site and has recently moved in with her. They are a match made in heaven and I am so pleased for him. It was worth every penny of the whole dating thing just for making a great new friend like Alan. I am yet to meet the man of my dreams from online dating, but Alan made me realise there are nice, normal men on the site.'
Annabel, 26, Leicester

Wife beater

'Simon* was really witty and a gent and we went on a good few dates, but something just wasn't quite right. While he was funny and clearly made an effort (I told him I liked Scrabble and the next date he bought a set just so we could play it in the pub), but a couple of things just kept bugging me. I don't think I'm shallow but I think most girls would find it hard to get over a boy wearing a wife beater vest in a non-ironic way. I just couldn't stop staring at those gross tufts of armpit hair poking out from under his arms! He also never ever drank, which is absolutely fine and admirable but it wasn't as if he was health-conscious. Instead, while I got slowly battered on my own on gin and tonics, he would cane the Red Bull and tell me about all the drugs he took when sitting at home on his own. It didn't seem congruous to me that he would steer clear of booze but be happy to get tanked

up on far worse substances! Frankly it was a real turn off and that was that really.' Anne, 31, Wigan

Wrong first time

'I was a seasoned online dater by the time I met Rick*. I'd had excellent dates, mediocre dates and downright dull dates. But this time I lived out every online dater's fear – not recognising him and approaching someone else right in front of him.

We had agreed to meet at a pub and by email he had sounded promising. He was witty, didn't use awful text speak and it sounded like we would get on well. I arrived at the pub and went up to who I thought was him and said hello. Blank face. Oh dear.

"You're not Rick?"

"No."

"Er – are you sure?"

"Yes! Not Rick."

(sheepish) "Oh – sorry! I thought you were someone else."

I looked around the pub and saw someone else that at a push could've been him: "No, love, no idea who you are but I'll have a date wiv yer if you like."

I approached around four different men (this is a small, quiet pub and people are starting to look) and am on the point of just giving up when man number one sniggers and beckons me over. It had been my date after all and he just wanted to watch me squirm. I mean *really! Mild social humiliation is hardly the way to a girl's heart. Still, I was there and thought I would give him another shot. That night a pub quiz was on so we settled down in a corner to show off our trivia masterminds. Again, it went horribly wrong. He knew I had more qualifications than him and had a go at me for not knowing the answers to more questions (I didn't study the names of tube stations at university, funnily enough). Even the way he wrote was aggressive. He clutched the pen with such might that the table shook and spilled my drink. He seemed bored, angry, aggressive, pretty much everything you don't want to be when you're trying to impress someone.*

Needless to say the night dragged and by the time the end of the quiz came round I was very ready to go. We parted, I waved (not even a peck) and I set about texting my friends about the surprise mentalist I'd just met. You can imagine my utter surprise when I had an email from him the next morning saying what a marvellous time he'd had, how he was actually shy and that he was sorry for the mean trick he'd played on me at the beginning of the date. By that point in my online dating career (if you can call it that) I had become a lot more ruthless – I told him politely but firmly that there wouldn't be another date and advised him for future ones with other girls to tone it all down a bit. And admit who he was when she introduced herself!' Natalie, 28, Kent

Perseverance works

'I had a couple of dates – not disastrous – but nothing setting my world alight and then my third date turned out to be The One. However, this was not before I had received an email from someone who can best be described as a beardie-weirdie geography teacher type, old enough to be my grandfather (despite the fact I had specified an age range of 30–40). His email started out fairly tame, saying how he liked the sound of my profile and that my photo looked nice. Despite this being his very first contact with me, the email very quickly turned on to sex and he said that there was no point in beating around the bush, that he loved sex and wanted to learn very quickly about how we could please each other inside and outside the bedroom. That together with the beardie-weirdie image was enough to make me log off and be too traumatised to log on again for a month!

Another email I received was from a man who had clearly swallowed a dictionary. Why use one word when 300 will do? Again, it was the first email, the purpose of which is usually to hook people in and encourage them to respond. However, his email ran to about five pages and seemed to use some sort of code. He kept referring to llamas in the back garden (despite neither my profile or his making any reference to either). My friends and I decided this may be some sort of code for him liking anal sex!

It's just as well I didn't let any of this put me off or I wouldn't be so happy with my perfect man now!'
Amanda, 29, Gloucester

Left out in the cold

'Strangely, one of the best dates I ever went on was spent sitting on the stairs in the hall outside my flat in the dark with someone I didn't even fancy!

I met up with Michael* in a pub one afternoon between Christmas and New Year. Having spent most of our Christmas break emailing each other to seek salvage from our respective family festivities we had built up quite a rapport, so I was disappointed to discover that I just wasn't attracted to Michael in person. However, I wasn't at all fazed by the idea of spending the afternoon with him, as I knew we got on and he looked like a good sort. He certainly proved himself on that front.

About half an hour into the date I went to get my wallet out of my bag to buy a round only to discover my bag had been stolen. To make matters worse I suddenly realised that I had a Christmas card in there with my address on – as well as my keys. As my flatmate wouldn't be home from work for hours, the only way I could be sure we wouldn't get burgled was to go and sit outside the flat for three hours – in the freezing cold.

Michael, who had spent the last ten minutes wandering the street searching bins for my bag, laughed when I told him and said it was no problem. I told him not to be ridiculous, that he should go home, but he insisted on coming with me. He even offered me his coat and gloves.

As soon as we arrived at the flat, Michael disappeared then came back two minutes later with a bottle of champagne and two huge bars of Green & Black's chocolate (he knew it was my favourite). Luckily, somebody from the downstairs flat was in so she let us in on her way out. We then spent the next three hours sitting on the stairwell outside my flat eating chocolate, drinking champagne and playing silly games in the dark (we got bored of turning on the timer light every two minutes).

When my flatmate arrived back three hours later, I invited Michael in and cooked him dinner to say thanks. I felt terrible at the end of the evening when he tried to kiss me and I had to say that I only wanted to be friends. He said he was really disappointed but it didn't stop him from walking half an hour in the cold the next day to bring round his old phone for me to keep indefinitely. Why do I only seem to be attracted to the ones who don't call?'
Kelly, 21, Dorset

Killer heels

'When I texted my best mate to tell her I was going to wow my date that night with my new killer heels, little did I know how right I was. Let's just say one minute I was having a brilliant time with Greg*, the next minute I was waking up in a hospital having my nose stitched by a nurse. New high stilettos plus four cocktails equals disastrous date. I don't remember much about the accident because I had concussion but according to Greg, one minute we were kissing in the taxi queue, the next minute, I'd disappeared. I had stepped forwards and stumbled on the kerb, smacking my nose on the pavement. Poor Greg had taken me to casualty and waited with me for four hours to get seen and even held

my hand while I was having my nose stitched. That bit I could deal with, but the broken front tooth was not a good look. To my amazement Greg did call the next day and we went out for six months.' Tara, 21, Devon

Fancy seeing you here

'Shortly before I met my husband (through a friend) I decided to give online dating a go. I was very nervous about the whole thing and embarrassed to tell anyone so it was all done in secret. I met one guy, a TV director, who turned out to be quite nice. We had a couple of dates, the last one was on a Friday night and he insisted that we get together again that weekend. As he said goodbye he tried to kiss me on the lips and missed. We had arranged to see one another again on the Sunday but I never heard from him again. Well, that is until I met my now husband a few months after the online date. Three months into the relationship, he was on the phone and mentioned the online date's name. When he finished the phone call I quizzed him asking him about the person he'd mentioned on the phone. It turned out that my online date was a really good friend of his and had worked with him on a Channel 4 programme. I was really embarrassed about the whole thing and had to reveal how I'd met this guy, and even worse, had to meet him again a few weeks later in a pub. Unbelievably, when my husband went to the loo, he whispered to me "Oh well it would never have worked out as I'm always travelling!"' Rachel, 27, Bournemouth

King of the castle

'It took a while for me to make contact with someone tempting enough to meet in the flesh – and even longer to grow the balls to actually go through with meeting him. It turned out he was lovely and what's more, like a real-life Prince Charming, he owned a 'castle'! In fact, it was a tourist attraction not too far away from where I live. We had the most fabulous first date, which was a tour around his castle, lunch in his village followed by a very romantic walk with his dog in the rain. Things went incredibly well and he even asked me if I had any plans for Christmas. But sadly, it wasn't quite the fairytale ending I thought as he stood me up on our second date. Ah well, it's back to the keyboard for me!' Louise, 25, Kent

CHAPTER 13
Fairytale Endings

Still not convinced it's possible to meet Prince Charming online? Then don't take my word for it . . .

Gareth, 27 and Laura, 27

Laura: To begin with, I was highly scathing of the whole online dating business. I had assumed only freaks/ weirdos/mass murderers would be doing it and had always dismissed it out of hand. I was also worried that my friends might think I was desperate and that if a relationship came out of it, they'd see it in a different light to other relationships where the couple has met through friends/in a bar, etc. I think there's a certain stigma attached to the whole online-dating scene still, although people seem now to be gradually accepting it more. I think the traditional view is that you'll meet someone in a highly romantic way – eyes meeting across a crowded room, etc. but the truth is that hardly ever happens and just because you've gone about it in a slightly different way doesn't mean you've 'cheated' or diminished what you have.

After having thought about it for a while I also realised that, certainly with mysinglefriend, a lot of the people I saw on there seemed prepared to contemplate a relationship and were open to the idea. In that sense, I think online dating can be more fulfilling and successful than just meeting in a bar or other forms of dating, where you so often do not know what the other person is looking for.

I had moved to Oxford about a year before I signed up and had found it hard to meet new people. I had a few friends around the place but they all had partners and generally wanted to do coupley stuff. I took up a few new hobbies, but Pilates and jewellery-making don't seem to attract that many (hot) guys! I figured I had a couple of options opens to me: moving (which is a little extreme) or to give the whole online dating thing a go.

I hadn't been on MSF for long before Gareth and I started emailing. I'd only replied to one other guy's email and it was clear from the outset that that wasn't going anywhere – there was absolutely no spark and besides, he had a bit of a moon-like face (harsh, but true!).

I had also signed-up for, but not subscribed to, match.com, but I got the feeling it was quite impersonal. I had plenty of 'winks' (an equivalent to a Facebook poke) from guys I clearly had nothing in common with and who seemed to just be covering all options. A low point was a wink from a pretty grim-looking, portly truck-driver from Germany; his picture still haunts me to this day.

Gareth and I actually nearly didn't meet up. One of the 'perks' of the MSF site is being able to check whether someone has read your email to them. I knew he'd read one of my emails yet didn't reply for a week. I sent him another one, and still nothing so I swore to my best friend that I wouldn't reply if he did respond. Needless to say, he charmed me, my resolve crumbled (as usual) and I did.

My first thought when I saw Gareth was, 'Oooo he's lovely!' We clicked, which I thought we would from our emails, but you can never be sure about these things. I knew he was special straight away and he made me laugh lots, which is always a good sign.

I was very nervous when I arrived but Gareth put me at ease quite quickly. Although it was slightly embarrassing at first as I couldn't open the glass door to get into the bar, I felt like a right idiot but apparently he didn't notice. I felt a bit flustered for a bit, told him some embarrassing anecdotes from my childhood and then the G&T kicked in.

I hoped this was going to be the start of something but I still couldn't believe it when he called the next day like he said he would. Not because he seemed like some kind of pathological liar but speaking from experience, men often don't call when they say they will, if at all. My inkling was right anyway because we're now engaged. We're having a big, traditional country wedding in Summer 2010.

Gareth: Last November, after some awkward dates and unanswered emails with girls on mysingel-friend.com, I went for a drink with a young lady named

Laura. We spent an evening laughing at anecdotes involving vengeful French teachers, cabbage and the Oxford English Dictionary's editorial policy, and soon found ourselves dancing in each other's arms at a gig in London.

Nearly a year on, Laura is now living in my flat with me. A couple of weeks ago I got down on one knee to pop the question, and she said yes!

I never had a problem with the idea of internet dating, personally, although I did worry about what my friends would think. However, I know a number of other people who have met their partners in this way and that really helped me get over those worries. One of my best friends met his long-term girlfriend online two and a half years ago and they are now living together. And I know many other friends that have at least tried it.

I'd been on another site before MSF but had no joy on there, and then my flatmate signed me up. I immediately thought that the calibre of people on there was higher than elsewhere and threw myself into it wholeheartedly.

I spent a couple of months on the site before I met Laura, during which time I met two other girls and had emails to others ignored. During the only date with the first girl I met, conversation was very forced and awkward. I had one of those 'uhh, cheque please!' moments when she told me that besides Kung-Fu, her main hobby was 'Buffy the Vampire Slayer role-play'!

I met a couple of others – one who was a bit odd and another who was perfectly nice but in hindsight, not right for me. I 'pounced' on Laura almost as soon as she appeared on the site, and she replied pretty quickly. We spent three or four weeks emailing before I asked her out for a drink. Apparently she had almost resolved to cut off contact with me because I was being so slow to reply to her!

When we finally met up my very first impression was 'wow, this girl is even prettier than her photo', which I'm guessing is pretty rare in the online dating world as most people will choose their most flattering shot for their profile. Once we got chatting it became obvious to me that Laura was (and is!) a sweet, funny girl with a sarcastic wit and a similar silly sense of humour to my own. I'd made my mind up that I properly 'fancied' her within an hour or so!

I was aware that I think I was too nervous before other dates, and so resolved to go into this one with no expectations, almost as if I didn't care about the outcome. I had a drink before I left home to help me relax and that really helped me be myself. I credit my relaxed nature as being the reason that Laura was able to see the real me on our first date.

At the end of the date, I promised Laura I would phone her the next day and that we would arrange something for the coming week, but I didn't know any more than that. After our second date, I remember thinking, 'Yeah, this can definitely go somewhere good'. It was only after about 6 weeks that I realised that Laura was the person with whom I wanted to spend the rest of my life!

We're getting married in Summer 2010, somewhere near Oxford. We haven't decided on any details yet –

except we are having a choccie cake! Neither of us ever thought that our MSF experience would lead to us finding the perfect partner, but as a result of our early internet-based flirting we are now extraordinarily happy and looking forward to the rest of our lives by each other's side.

Tracy and Stu, Leeds

Tracy: I had tried internet dating a couple of years ago but hadn't had much luck. It was a case of too short (yes, I am that shallow), too boring, too old, too weird . . . the usual stories. So I stopped for a while and met a couple of guys in real life. Then in September 2007 I found myself single again and decided to give it another try. I'd just started living on my own for the first time and on the other side of town from all my friends. So I guess I felt a bit lonely and thought it might be a good way of just getting out and also having a confidence boost.

This time I joined Guardian Soulmates. I thought this would be a good way to meet someone intelligent. One of the first guys to add me as a favourite was SPK. I looked at his profile and thought he looked cute and we had lots in common – especially music, as we'd both filled out that section more thoroughly than a lot of people. So I emailed him a short message just to say, 'Saw you'd added me as a favourite so thought I'd say hi. How was your weekend?' SPK replied and for about three days we emailed each other several times a day, our messages getting longer and longer. I was getting very excited to receive his emails which I hadn't done with other guys, his messages made me laugh and I couldn't believe how much we had in common – music, films, pretty much everything clicked. I was waiting for him to ask me out. Other guys had asked me out after a couple of messages but he was taking his time. So eventually I dropped a massive hint and emailed him my phone number saying it was so he could text me for a change from emailing if he wanted. He got the hint and a couple of texts later he asked if I wanted to meet up.

We met on a Thursday night, at a bar in Leeds. I was ridiculously nervous, more nervous that I had been meeting others dates previously because I hadn't been on a date in a while, and I think I knew we were going to get on so well. I decided to be fashionably late (10 minutes of course) but my train ended up actually being late which just added to my stress levels and by the time I got there, almost 30 minutes later, I was all flustered and bright red. Turns out he'd arrived far too early and had been sitting in the bar waiting for me for the best part of an hour. My first impression was that he was much fitter than he was in any of his profile pictures, and luckily he was as tall as he'd said in his profile. He'd already got us a bottle of wine and so we sat in the window of this bar and just chatted and drank. We got on brilliantly and ended up drinking another couple of bottles before the date was over. He told me he liked to cook and so I (drunkenly) invited myself over to his that Sunday night so he could cook me a Thai green curry. At some point in the night I nipped to the toilet and texted my friend saying, 'He's really cute, smart and funny. We have loads in common and I really like him. Definitely think we're going to meet up again. He's quality!' I later found out at the same time he texted his mate saying, 'She's fit.'

The best thing about meeting online is that it was all quite sweet and things happened in the right order, as opposed to when you meet someone in a bar and end up having a snog and a grope in a dark corner, then exchange phone numbers and arrange to meet up another night. Then when you do meet up you have that weird thing of, 'We've already kissed, but now I'm really nervous around you and don't know you.' Stu and I didn't even kiss until our second date so it all felt very sweet and lovely.

We don't think we would have met if it hadn't been for online dating. We didn't hang out in the same places, and even if we had ended up in the same bar at some point, Stu reckons he never would have approached me, and I know I wouldn't have chatted him up. His parents don't know we met on a dating website though – he vaguely mentioned that we'd met through the internet and his Mum said, 'Facebook?' and he just said, 'Yeah, something like that.' Although we got engaged on Christmas Eve and so I have a feeling the story of how we met might be mentioned at some point when we get married in October!

Amie, 25 and Ben, 30

Amie: Ben had only been online dating for a week when he added me to his favourites. I was actually online at the time, and I liked what I saw, so I added him to mine immediately.

His first message was different to others' 'what you up to this weekend?' type emails, which I found refreshing. Three hours later we were still messaging and not running out of things to talk about.

We had our first date the following weekend and haven't looked back. We've been together three months now and we going on holiday to The Gambia together in February. Neither of us has been this happy in ages.

Several of my friends and work colleagues were in happy relationships because of online dating so I was open minded when I signed up. My motto was 'what have you got to lose.' There isn't the stigma attached anymore, it's the done thing. To me it seems like a far more controlled way of meeting people rather than ending up chatting to someone in a bar or club. With the internet you can (this sounds really bad) window shop and suss people out to a certain extent before you decide to meet up.

I first went on the site for free for a month (no messaging) and then paid up in full and had been messaging people for about two weeks before I met Ben. In that time I had email contact with about 20 men. I went on two dates, one with a very sweet guy, but as soon as we met I knew there was going to be no romance on my part. The second guy was OK but again, I knew that we wouldn't be seeing each other again. They were both what you'd expect, a little bit uncomfortable, and I was clock-watching thinking what is an acceptable length of time to stay on this date! It sounds like a cliché but you just know – must be female intuition . . .

Ben's emails were very chatty in an intelligent, fun and friendly kind of way. We had lots in common and happily whiled away a Saturday afternoon messaging each other. The emails got longer and longer to the point where they were about three pages long. There was some banter (mainly about my job and the stereotypes). Ben was very complimentary in his emails but the flirting began in earnest on both parts via text a few days before we met up.

When Ben and I met up I do have to 'fess up to hitting the alcohol straight away and caning the majority of a bottle of wine – but just for Dutch courage!

I was a bit nervous but we had been emailing for a week and the majority of that week we had chatted for a few hours each night on the phone. I knew we would have plenty to talk about and things wouldn't be awkward.

We met at his house (I know that's a massive no-no but never mind!), went into Leicester and had some lunch and a few beers and wandered around the city. It was a red-hot day so we then sat in the garden chatting for most of the afternoon. By this point I had had far too much to drink so ended up staying over (again a massive no-no but I'm still alive and we're still together so what the hell?). And just for the record, nothing happened, Ben was the perfect gentleman!

Ben: I'd been in email contact with a couple of people before Amie but nothing really happened. It was all fairly boring run of the mill conversation and most of it was either a bit of a turn off or made me feel 100 years old ('What's your favourite colour?', 'What's your star sign?',

'Are you going to Ibiza on holiday this year? I am and it's going to be amazing' . . .).

I didn't go on any dates with anyone through the site but I went on a couple of dates with someone outside of the site for about four weeks up until a month or so before I met Amie. It turned into more of a friendship than a relationship, which wasn't what either of us were looking for so we broke it off and went our separate ways.

I was a bit unsure what to expect with online dating, but I had a couple of friends who had tried before with varying success so thought I'd give it a go. My biggest concern was people I knew spotting me online and what they would then think of me. I got over that one pretty quickly though.

I finally took the plunge after too much wine one night. Plus, a friend bought me a subscription. She was going travelling and decided I needed someone to look after me!

The second we met up I thought it must be Christmas. Amie looked amazing in her profile photographs. However, I've since learned she looks way better in person. She's absolutely gorgeous and I still haven't got over that wow-factor the first time I see her after a week apart.

Despite that, I wasn't really nervous on the first date. I'm usually quite quiet and shy initially, but weirdly enough having chatted so much before we met up (tens of emails, five or six phone calls all well over an hour long, and so many text messages – I could do push-ups with my thumbs!) the nerves had pretty much all gone. Having said that, I did spill quite a bit of wine that afternoon!

I knew for definite on that first date it was going to be the start of something. I knew I really liked Amie before we met; I've always put a lot of emphasis on character and personality. We instantly had so much to talk about, lots of back and forth chat (about nothing most of the time) and really similar values and views. I was really looking forward to spending time with Amie, I just hoped she felt the same way about me. Luckily she did!

We're really looking forward to our holiday to Gambia and are also looking at going away later in the year. I can't remember clicking with someone so quickly, or ever being so happy.

Sabine, 25 and Matt, 29

Sabine: I was really unsure about the idea of paying to find a date – I didn't think girls had to do that, but I was sick of meeting the same type of man in a bar and didn't know how else I was going to meet a great guy. Plus, I like the idea of finding out a bit about someone before getting involved and I thought that if guys went to the trouble of having a profile written up and paying to date they must be quite serious about meeting someone special, too.

Matt was the first man I sent a message to on mysinglefriend.com. We chatted a little but didn't go into too much detail. Because we didn't overly bond by email I wasn't sure how chatty he was going to be. I certainly didn't think we'd click the way we did.

I was speaking to a couple of other guys on the site who really sold themselves by email, but Matt seemed very formal and straight to the point. He later said that he doesn't see the point of chatting too much by email, it's better to meet sooner rather than later if you like the look of each other, which I think is very true. You might click by email but have no spark in real life, in which case you're left disappointed and have wasted time chatting to somebody unsuitable.

I laugh about it now but I told Matt afterwards that I almost didn't meet him as I thought he came across slightly arrogant (which couldn't be further from the truth). I really liked the recommendation on his profile by his best friend's girlfriend Donna and I thought he was cute so thought I'd give him a chance. I had no idea I'd be meeting an absolute sweetheart though.

Matt had only just moved up to Manchester from Southampton and was literally moving all his stuff into his new apartment when we started chatting. He suggested meeting up for a drink on the third email which I thought was quite forward but I liked it. Too many guys try and charm girls by chatting on email by which point another guy has probably already met them and snapped them up.

There was a spark instantly. He made me feel at ease and we had a lovely evening, I hadn't laughed that much for a long time. Our date lasted until about 1.30am (on a work night!) which was a positive sign.

Our second date went well – we had our first kiss – but we really clicked on the following Sunday. We went for a meal and a night out with my brother and his girlfriend. Matt and I ended up staying up all night, chatting and getting to know each other.

He then surprised me by taking me to London for two days, which was one of the best breaks of my life. We were totally smitten by then. Matt spoiled me rotten with meals, cocktails, Madame Tussauds and the stage production of *Dirty Dancing*, my favourite film of all time.

I hadn't been on many internet dates before that, only a couple of fun dating applications on Facebook, and I'd never met anyone who exactly blew me away. I've had three long-term relationships before Matt and was on the dating scene in between. I've had to kiss a few frogs before finding him!

I never expected to find my perfect man on an internet dating site but I did, and he was my first and only date. It was definitely the best money I've ever spent!

Jodi and Andy, Andover

Jodi: I had been on my own for three years and was on the verge of moving the children and me into a convent, so I thought it was time to give internet dating a go! All my friends thought I was nutty, apart from my best friend who recommended me to the site.

Andy wrote to me first. In his picture he had his mouth closed (his mean and moody look he said), so I was worried he didn't have any teeth. I had my photo taken sitting on some stairs and he said it looked like I was on a Stannah stair lift. Thankfully, neither of us make decisions based on looks!

Andy had emailed five or six other girls at the same time he wrote to me but I hadn't been brave enough to contact anyone. We emailed for two weeks. They started off quite light-hearted and generic for the first week, then got more flirty. We then spoke on the phone for a week and then finally met up.

We met halfway between our homes in a pub in Basingstoke. Andy wasn't nervous but I was absolutely terrified. My friends were texting and calling every 10 minutes as they were convinced he was a serial killer. At first, I thought he was disappointed. I also found it hard to merge the person sitting in front of me with the one I had been talking to – only for the first hour though. Within about an hour we both knew it was going to work, but neither of us can put our finger on why. We had drinks and dinner then sat in the car until 4 am chatting. Neither of us wanted to leave.

Six months later Andy moved 42 miles to live with me, we got engaged last October, and seven weeks ago our beautiful daughter Sophie was born. I'd almost given up hope of meeting anyone as I already had children from my previous relationship and been single for three years, but I've been lucky enough to meet the most wonderful, wonderful man who loves my children as much as I do. We're both happier than we've ever been.

People are not always understanding when they find out you're looking online, but our story proves that it can be hugely successful. Living so far apart means that without this form of dating we would never have met.

CHAPTER 14

A Few Words About Safety

Okay, this may not be the most scintillating chapter of the book but it's an important one, so at the risk of sounding like your mum, please do read these words of advice on keeping safe. You're not stupid, you know what you're doing, you'd be able to smell a nutter a mile away, that kind of thing would never happen to you . . . yes, yes, but let's face it, love, lust and alcohol can be a lethal cocktail potent enough to make even the most grounded young lady take temporary leave of her senses. Here's how to date with your head as well as your heart.

Online safety

Don't put any personal details on your profile that could enable somebody to trace you. That includes your mobile, home and work number, your home or work address, any of your email addresses, the name of the company you work for or even the name of any of your local haunts.

Use the site's own internal email system. All reputable dating sites should have one (if in doubt, choose one of the recommended sites in Chapter 2). This enables you to communicate anonymously with fellow daters without giving away your personal details.

Don't give out your personal email address or phone number over email until you have spent some time getting to know the person. If you do need to communicate to organise a date, it may be worth setting up a separate free email account such as Google, Hotmail or Yahoo.

Don't ever feel pressured into giving someone your personal details. Any man worth dating should respect your safety concerns. If he continues to cajole you into giving out your phone number, you might want to reconsider whether this is the kind of man you really want to meet up with alone.

The moment you feel uncomfortable, intimidated or suspicious about someone, report him to the site moderators. Most sites also have a facility that enables you to 'block' people from contacting you.

Look out for the warning signs:

- He's evasive with your questions.
- He contradicts himself.
- He's keen to know your personal details.
- He wants to meet you at your place or his.
- His emails are inconsistent or unpredictable.
- He doesn't sound genuine.

On the date

Ideally, the first date should be short, sweet, alcohol-free and in daylight hours. Lunch or a coffee is always a sensible option (plus it gives you the opportunity to leg it if the chemistry isn't there).

If you're meeting him on your lunch break from work, arrange to hook up somewhere away from the office. If you weren't getting the right vibes on the date and he insists on walking you back to work, have an excuse ready that you need to pop to the post office on the way back.

Arrange to meet in a busy, well-lit public place. Do *not* arrange to meet at his place or yours – whatever the reason. Avoid meeting in your local too. The less information you give away prior to the date the better. This might sound over-zealous but it's always better to be safe than sorry.

Try to stick with a venue that you already know, have heard of or feel comfortable with or if he's made a suggestion, check it out online to make sure it's not some seedy hang-out down a back alley.

Give the details of what time you're meeting up, where you're going and the name and number of your date to a couple of friends and have them keep an eye on their phone. Arrange to text them at a certain time to say you're okay and at the end of the night to let them know you got home safely.

Don't forget to take your phone – fully charged!

Even if you're having an amazing time and he seems like the perfect gentleman, remember that he is still a virtual stranger. Some guys know how to get exactly what they want by playing the charmer routine. Take it one step at a time. Never let your date pressure you into staying out, having another drink, moving on somewhere you don't know, going back to his.

Ideally, get a cab back home and be the one to get out last if you're sharing. He doesn't need to know your address right now.

You should be in control at all times so DON'T drink too much. Only you know your threshold, so remind yourself when you arrive and stick to it. If you start to feel drunk, switch to soft drinks. If he's any kind of man worth dating, he'll respect that and won't try to persuade you otherwise.

If you do meet a dodgy character, or feel suspicious about someone, report them immediately to the site for the safety of the other girls on the site.

Let's talk about sex

Even if you fancy the pants off him, it's a wise idea to keep yours firmly on until you've built up some trust. As I said in the introduction of this book, I'm not here to preach to you about how many dates you should wait before you sleep with someone. Only you will know when the time is right. But just be aware that your judgement goes out of the window after a few wines, and *always* use a condom.